MW01536355

THE POCKET IDIOT'S GUIDE TO

America's Golf Courses

by Rich Mintzer

alpha
books

A Division of Macmillan Reference USA
A Simon and Schuster Macmillan Company
1633 Broadway New York, NY 10019-6785

This book is dedicated to golf course architects who allow us to enjoy the wealth of unique, challenging designs that make this game so great.

©1999 by Rich Mintzer

International Standard Book Number: 0-02-862944-2
Library of Congress Catalog Card Number: 98-89800

01 00 99   4 3 2 1

Interpretation of the printing code: The rightmost number of the first series of numbers is the year of the book's printing; the rightmost number of the second series of numbers is the number of the book's printing. For example, a printing code of 99-1 shows that the first printing occurred in 1999.

Printed in the United States of America

Publisher: Kathy Nebenhaus
Editorial Director: Gary M. Krebs
Managing Editor: Bob Shuman
Marketing Brand Manager: Felice Primeau
Development Editors: Phil Kitchel, Amy Zavatto
Development Editor: Nancy Warner
Production Editor: Christina Van Camp
Copy Editor: Kris Simmons
Cover Designer: Mike Freeland
Photo Editor: Richard H. Fox
Illustrator: Kevin Spear
Designer: Scott Meola
Indexer: Angie Bess
Layout/Proofreading: Angela Calvert, Julie Trippetti

Contents

Introduction

Golf is the fastest growing game in America today, with millions of players taking to 16,000 courses nationwide. From duffers to low handicappers, the game is a weekend pastime for some, a great place to handle outdoor business transactions for others, and simply a way of life to the serious devotees.

This guide serves as a source for courses in and around several major markets. We've included both resort and public courses as well as a few excellent courses that you can play when visiting any one of several areas throughout the country. The courses range from urban municipal layouts that offer primarily no-frills golf in easily accessible locations to five-star resorts outside the downtown business sections that put you in the lap of luxury with first-class service. Most resort courses listed do not require you to be a guest of the hotel. Guests, however, have special privileges, including golf packages, advance tee-time reservation capabilities, free driving-range benefits, and so on.

No matter where you choose to play, because of the popularity of the game, it's wise to plan in advance. From 24 hours to a year ahead, courses take tee time advance bookings. Many require a credit card, so have one handy when dialing. Many will have a cancellation policy (listed where available). It's always worth asking. Some courses allow you to prepay on a credit card. While making your tee time reservation (especially when prepaying on your credit card), inquire about what happens in the event of rain.

Many courses will list two phone numbers. Often the 800 or 888 toll-free number is for tee times and room reservations (where applicable). The local area number will more than likely get you to the pro shop where you can get some questions answered prior to making your tee time reservation. In addition to advance tee time requirements, locations, and phone numbers, the listings offer a brief description of the courses. Mentions of hills, water, sand, bunkers, ravines, elevation changes (meaning down from tees or up to greens), and other aspects of a course prepare you for the type of layout you will be playing. Links-style courses are spread out with rolling fairways (small hills throughout) and dunes and mounds. They are usually off the shoreline and involve a wind factor. The links-style courses, which originated with the earliest courses in Scotland, are usually wide open and very challenging. Tight courses are those characterized with either woods or hazards lining the fairways, forcing you to hit the ball straight. *Target golf* is a term used to describe what you play on many of these courses because if you stray off the fairway, you'll be searching for your ball. Small greens are (obviously) harder to hit, whereas large greens challenge you not to three-putt. Bent-grass greens are usually a fast, high-quality green.

The yardage listed for each course is from the front tees (often the ladies tees) and the back tees, or *tips*. Many golfers will choose one of the sets of tees in between, although a lot of us shift as we go, moving forward if our game isn't what we hoped it would be or back if the day is going well and we're seeking a greater challenge. Closer and shorter doesn't always mean the course is easier. The angles may change, and forced carries (where you *must* clear a hazard) may be equally or more difficult.

Par is usually the same from the various tees, although on some courses, you will see it vary. For example, a listing of 73/72 means that par is 73 from the women's tees and 72 from the men's and the championship tees. Colors of tee markers and names of tee areas may change, but the basic idea of choosing the one that suits you remains the same. Don't try to be a big shot and hit from the back tees if it's going to ruin your game and slow down those behind you.

All green fees listed in this book are subject to change—most likely increasing. Fees vary according to weekday or weekend and can also change according to the season. Many areas have peak season and off-season rates with a *shoulder season* in between. Some courses have different rates almost monthly. The range will give you an idea of whether you're looking at a $25 public facility or a $250-per-round top resort course in Las Vegas or Pebble Beach. Some of the higher-end courses include golf carts with computerized yard markers, and some courses feature the new concept of a *forecaddie*, who is essentially someone who guides you around the course.

Keep in mind that the most popular playing times are early in the day, particularly on weekends, which are the most crowded days. You might take advantage of a late afternoon playing time and in many cases enjoy a lower *twilight* rate. If you hit the course at 3 p.m., you can usually finish a round by 7 or 7:30 p.m. Also note that 9-hole rates are not listed, but some courses will allow you to play nine for less money. If you're older than 60 or 65 (depending on the course), ask about a senior discount.

One of the facilities included in the listings is the clubhouse, which can range from small waiting areas to elaborate settings with restaurants and banquet facilities. Pro shops, driving ranges, chipping areas, and putting greens are also listed. Restaurants and snack bars are mentioned as well. Some courses also offer beverage carts, which are essentially refreshments on various locations along the course itself.

Where applicable, hotel packages are included. Resorts have golf packages available, whereas other courses may have discounts or packages offered with local hotels. In the more golf-centered (vacation) areas, such as Phoenix/Scottsdale, Orlando, Miami, Hilton Head, or Las Vegas, the hotel concierges at most major area locations will be able to assist you with tee times and directions. In some major cities, particularly in the Northeast, such as New York, you might have to fend for yourself because the courses are all outside of the downtown area.

The listings to follow will give you a few courses from which to choose when hitting a major market for business or pleasure. Good luck, and happy golfing!

Acknowledgments

I'd like to thank Mary Colleen Liburdi at Audubon International, Chad Ritterbusch, the American Society of Golf Course Architects, as well as several members, including Geoffery Cornish and the people at Mike Hurdzan Design, among others. Also thank you to all the people who were helpful in providing information for the book, including Jim Abbott in Cincinnati, Mike Smith in Portland, and many more. Also a big thank you to Alan Wasserman for a lot of help, to my wife Carol, to Lou Spiazzi, and to the man who's played the Top 100, Bernie Hiller. And finally, thanks, Gary, Nancy, Chris, and Kris.

Atlanta

Atlantic City

Atlanta

The Atlanta area boasts more than 70 public and resort courses. Area course superintendents take great pride in Bermuda fairways and bent-grass greens with tree-lined fairways. The courses are not usually difficult to get on with some advance booking, and most sit outside of the city—or in the perimeter as it's referred to—within 30 minutes of downtown. The resorts feature old-fashioned Southern charm and courses in natural settings. Golfers hit the courses practically year-round.

Bradshaw Farm Golf Club
3030 Bradshaw Club Drive, Woodstock, GA 30188
Atlanta, GA
770-592-2222
Public

This new public facility overlooks the city of Atlanta and then some. The long course offers dramatic elevation changes, including a couple of 100-yard drops from tee to fairway.

(Bradshaw Farm Golf Club cont'd)

Hilly terrain, tight tree-lined fairways, water on 14 holes, views of the North Georgia Mountains, a meandering creek, Bermuda fairways, bent-grass greens, and a farm motif are all part of Bradshaw.

Yardage: 4,700 to 6,800 / 4 sets of tees

Par: 72

Open: Year-round

Tee times: Up to 7 days in advance

Green fees: $45 weekdays, $65 weekends, including cart

Facility includes: Unique barn clubhouse, pro shop, driving range, putting green, restaurant

Packages with Renaissance Waverly in Atlanta.

Callaway Gardens Resort
U.S. Highway 27, Pine Mountain, GA 31822-2000
706-663-2281
Resort

In the Columbus area, 90 minutes south of Atlanta, Callaway is a popular resort for meetings, conventions, and corporate tournaments. Three 18-hole courses include the Garden View, which features wide fairways and challenging greens surrounded by a couple dozen bunkers in a picturesque setting. Lake View is aptly named because you'll find water almost everywhere on this tough shorter course. The long Mountain View course offers tight tree-lined fairways plus two lakes and a classic par 5 15th hole. The Mountain View course is home to the PGA Buick Challenge.

Yardage: Garden View, 5,848 to 6,392; Lake View, 5,452 to 6,006; Mountain View, 5,848 to 7,057 / 3 sets of tees each

Par: Garden View, 72; Lake View, 71/70; Mountain View, 74/72

Open: Year-round

Tee times: Up to 72 hours in advance or when making hotel reservations

Green fees: Mountain View, seasonal from $70 to $100, including cart; Lake View and Garden View, seasonal from $55 to $75, including cart

Facility includes: Clubhouse, pro shop, driving range, putting greens, restaurants

Deluxe golf package available with resort.

Champions Club of Atlanta
15135 Hopewell Road, Alpharetta, GA 30004
770-343-9700
Public

As a fairly new course just 30 minutes north of Atlanta, Champions Club attracts a lot of players at all skill levels. Rolling hills, Bermuda fairways, fast bent-grass greens, and a couple of water holes in a naturally wooded area provide a solid round of golf in a well-maintained, low-key, relaxing environment.

Yardage: 6,300 to 6,725 / 4 sets of tees

Par: 72

Open: Year-round

Tee times: Up to 5 days in advance

Green fees: $55 to $69, including cart

Facility includes: Clubhouse, pro shop, driving range, putting green, full-service grill

Chateau Elan Winery and Resort
100 Tour de France, Braselton, GA 30517
800-233-9463
www.chateauelan.com
Resort / Public

About 30 minutes from Atlanta is one of Georgia's most distinct resorts, Chateau Elan. In a suburb country-club–like atmosphere, the Chateau offers 63 holes of golf with two

(Chateau Elan Winery and Resort cont'd)

18-hole designs and one 9-hole course for guests and non-guests of the hotel. The Chateau course is a long winding layout that plays around two creeks and three lakes with 87 bunkers. Bermuda fairways and thick roughs lead to bent-grass greens. The Woodlands course is tree-lined and features numerous elevation changes and rolling hills. A third members-only course is open to resort guests on an availability-only basis. A short, par 3, 9-holer rounds out the golf portion of the vast landscape.

Yardage: Chateau, 5,900 to 7,300 / 3 sets of tees; Woodlands, 4,850 to 6,851 / 4 sets of tees

Par: Chateau, 71; Woodlands, 72

Open: Year-round

Tee times: Up to 7 days in advance, 30 days in advance for resort guests

Green fees: Seasonal from $50 to $75, including cart

Facility includes: Clubhouse, pro shop, driving range, chipping and pitching area, putting green, restaurant, snack shop, winery

Resort packages available.

Cobblestone Golf Course
4200 Nance Road, Acworth, GA 30101
770-917-5151
Public

One of the most popular courses in the Atlanta area (20 miles north), Cobblestone features 9 of its 18 holes along Lake Acworth in a picturesque layout. Undulating fairways and greens typify this consistently top-rated course, which offers a wide variety of holes, including some top-notch par 3s. With a demanding layout, this course is not recommended for new players.

Yardage: 5,300 to 6,759 / 4 sets of tees

Par: 71

Open: Year-round

Tee times: Up to 4 days in advance

Green fees: Seasonal from $52 to $59, including cart

Facility includes: Clubhouse, pro shop, driving range, putting green, grill

---

Olde Atlanta Golf Club
5750 Olde Atlanta Parkway, Suwanee, GA 30024
770-497-0097
Semi-Private

Olde in name only, the 1993 course sits only 15 miles northeast of Atlanta. Tree-lined fairways, elevation changes, water on a few holes, and bent-grass greens highlight this very well-maintained course, which will test all aspects of your game.

Yardage: 5,081 to 6,789 / 4 sets of tees

Par: 71

Open: Year-round

Tee times: Up to 7 days in advance

Green fees: $58 to $70, including cart

Facility includes: Clubhouse, pro shop, driving range, chipping area, 2 putting greens, restaurant

---

Riverpines Golf Club
4775 Old Alabama Road, Alpharetta, GA 30022
770-442-5960
Public

Only 30 minutes from Atlanta, Riverpines lies along the Chatahoochie River and brings water into play on more than half of the holes. Not a particularly long course, Riverpines has a lot to offer players at all levels. Bermuda fairways through rolling hills lead to fast bent-grass greens that will test your putting game. Spend some time on their excellent practice facilities as well.

(Riverpines Golf Club cont'd)

Yardage: 4,279 to 6,511 / 4 sets of tees

Par: 70

Open: Year-round

Tee times: Call Monday for the week

Green fees: $50 weekdays, $56 weekends, including cart

Facility includes: Clubhouse, pro shop, driving range, chipping area, 2 putting greens, par 3 course

---

Stouffer Pineisle Resort
9000 Holiday Road, Lake Lanier Islands, GA 30518
770-945-8921
Resort / Public

A popular destination for corporate meetings and conventions, the first-class Stouffer Pineisle Resort features a challenging 18 holes of golf. With a scenic backdrop of the Blue Ridge Mountains, the course offers hilly terrain, wooded rough, and enough bunkers to keep you on your toes. Eight holes border on water, so bring extra balls.

Yardage: 5,099 to 6,514 / 4 sets of tees

Par: 72

Open: Year-round

Tee times: Up to 7 days in advance or when booking reservation for guests

Green fees: $49 weekdays, $59 weekends, including cart

Facility includes: Clubhouse, pro shop, driving range, chipping area, putting green, golf pavilion, full-service restaurant

Various packages with resort.

Whitewater Country Club
175 Buckdale Drive, Fayetteville, GA 30215
770-461-6545
Semi-Private

Growing in popularity, this Arnold Palmer signature course is tighter on the front nine and wider open on the back. Bent-grass greens are kept in excellent condition on this challenging, somewhat secluded course, only 30 miles south of Atlanta.

Yardage: 4,909 to 6,739 / 4 sets of tees

Par: 72

Open: Year-round

Tee times: Up to 3 days in advance

Green fees: $38.85 Monday through Thursday, $49.35 Friday through Sunday, including cart

Facility includes: Clubhouse, pro shop, driving range, putting green, restaurant

Atlantic City

Atlantic City has been home to golf since the Atlantic City Country Club opened its doors in 1897. A number of classic old courses, both resort and public, are open for play within 20 minutes of the casino action. Most courses get very crowded during spring and summer months, so advance reservations are a must. Ask about cancellation policies. You can use any number of local golf-package companies.

For one-stop shopping, the Greater Atlantic City Golf Association (GACGA) has established a phone number, 800-GOLF222, that allows you to book on several area courses up to 13 months in advance. Courses may offer special discounts; check with them individually. The GACGA is also affiliated with 20 area hotel properties, but you need to contact the hotels for their own special packages. Area hotels try hard to accommodate your golfing needs. Groups can also call 888-CAPETRIP.

Blue Heron Pines Golf Club
550 West Country Club Drive, Calogne, NJ 08213
609-965-4653
www.blueheronpines.com
Public

The highly rated Blue Heron, with 18 distinctive holes, has been compared to the finest courses at Myrtle Beach. Only 15 minutes from the casino action, tight-rolling fairways and large greens highlight the popular, difficult course that is home to a wide variety of trees and a wider variety of birds. A new, second course, Blue Heron East will open in 2000.

Yardage: 5,053 to 6,777 / 5 sets of tees

Par: 72

Open: Year-round

Tee times: Up to 5 days in advance

Green fees: Seasonal from $51 to $125, including cart

Facility includes: Clubhouse, pro shop, driving range, chipping area, putting green, restaurant

Brigantine Golf Links
Roosevelt Boulevard and the Bay, Brigantine, NJ 08203
609-266-1388
Public

A distinctive Scottish links layout, Brigantine dates back to 1927. Tight fairways and plenty of water (on 14 of 18 holes) plus marshlands encourage you to hit accurately. The wind can also play havoc on this fun seaside course. Brigantine is the closest course to the casino action, only two miles north.

Yardage: 6,233 to 6,529 / 3 sets of tees

Par: 72

Open: Year-round

Tee times: Up to 5 days in advance

Green fees: Seasonal from $30 to $60, including cart

Facility includes: Clubhouse, pro shop, putting and chipping area, restaurant

Discount packages with several resorts.

Cape May National Golf Club
834 Florence Avenue, Erma, NJ 08204
609-884-1563
Public

This nearly 7,000-yard course is a test for anyone as it winds its way through plenty of trees with tight narrow fairways. Add water, and you have one of the most challenging courses in South Jersey. Well worth the 35-minute ride from the casino action, Cape May is a well-run facility with a spectacular finishing hole flanked by water with a green surrounded by trees.

Yardage: 4,711 to 6,905 / 5 sets of tees

Par: 71

Open: Year-round

Tee times: Up to 7 days in advance (not affiliated with GACGA)

Green fees: Seasonal from $35 to $75, including cart

Facility includes: Clubhouse, pro shop, state-of-the-art driving range, putting green, bar and grill

Affiliated with several hotels and inns.

Greate Bay Resort and Country Club
901 Mays Landing, Somers Point, NJ 08244
609-927-0066
Resort / Public

This classic old-links style course, only 10 minutes south of Atlantic City, offers a variety of holes in a traditional layout. Winds from the bay will make you rethink your strategy as

(Greate Bay Resort and Country Club cont'd)

you work around plenty of trees and several water holes onto large greens. The 160-acre facility provides a private club atmosphere and is popular with the casino crowd.

Yardage: 5,650 to 6,840 / 3 sets of tees

Par: 71

Open: Year-round

Tee times: Up to 5 days in advance

Green fees: Seasonal from $40 to $95, including cart

Facility includes: Clubhouse, pro shop, driving range, putting green, restaurant

---

Harbor Pines Golf Club
500 St. Andrews Drive, Egg Harbor Township, NJ 08234
609-926-9006
Public

One of the top-rated courses in New Jersey, Harbor Pines sits in a picturesque 520-acre setting and offers a quiet diversion from gaming excitement. Generous fairways, a dozen water hazards, well-situated wooded areas, plenty of sand, and large greens typify the Egg Harbor course.

Yardage: 5,099 to 6,827 / 5 sets of tees

Par: 72

Open: Year-round

Tee times: Up to 8 days in advance

Green fees: Seasonal (7-tiered structure) from $52 to $105, including cart

Facility includes: Clubhouse, pro shop, driving range, putting green

Marriott's Seaview Resort
401 South New York Road, Abescon, NJ 08201
609-748-7680
Resort / Public

One of the premier golf resorts in the area, Marriott offers conventioneers and business travelers fabulous accommodations, including course-side meeting facilities along two classic, old courses that have been home to many tournaments. The Bay course (along Reeds Bay) is a scenic wide-open old layout—not exceptionally long, but tricky with small greens. The neighboring Pines course is longer and tougher with very tight fairways lined by pine trees and a healthy amount of bunkers around large bent-grass greens. Marriott's Seaview is only 10 miles from Atlantic City.

Yardage: Pines, 5,276 to 6,731; Bay, 5,017 to 6,247 / 3 sets of tees each

Par: Bay, 71; Pines, 71

Open: Year-round

Tee times: Up to 7 days in advance, 30 days in advance for resort guests

Green fees: Seasonal from $80 to $125, including cart and forecaddie (your personal on-course assistant)

Facility includes: Clubhouse, pro shop, driving range, two chipping areas, putting, green, restaurant, snack bar

Packages with hotel include a round of golf per night stay; also packages with meetings.

Sand Barrens Golf Club
1765 Route 9 North, Swainton, NJ 08210
609-GOLF555
Public

This stunning new course offers tree-lined fairways, large greens, and plenty of water in lush, scenic surroundings. The

(Sand Barrens Golf Club cont'd)

very challenging, highly rated Sand Barrens appropriately has its share of sand as well. In spring 1999, Sand Barrens will expand to a 27-hole layout.

Yardage: 5,400 to 7,000 / 5 sets of tees

Par: 72

Open: Year-round

Tee times: Up to 7 days in advance, $20 premium rate for 6-month in-advance booking

Green fees: Seasonal from $39 to $85, including cart

Facility includes: Clubhouse forthcoming, pro shop, driving range, putting, green, snack bar

Special deals with local hotels.

Boston and New England

Boston and New England

Forget about playing in Boston; there just isn't room. From five miles away to the tip of Maine, you can enjoy any of hundreds of New England–style courses in the serene, country atmosphere that typifies the area. Many of the courses boarder on or overlook the ocean from the Cape Cod, Nantucket, and Martha's Vineyard region up the coast to Maine. Good luck making reservations in and around the Cape or Vineyard because many of these courses are hard to get on due to prepayment, memberships, and so on.

Because the New England area is dense with woodlands and flanked by magnificent mountains, there are no sprawling tracts of recently leveled landscapes prepped for two or three courses in one setting. Most layouts, therefore, fit comfortably within their natural surroundings, complete with elevation changes, trees, and wildlife. Several area courses date back many years. Top-rated resorts provide championship golf and all the other amenities in countrified settings—and if it's too cold to hit the course, you can ski on it in the winter.

Ideally, golf can be played from March through November, but that depends on the weather. The resort and vacation communities are helpful in arranging golf outings, but in the larger cities, you may get further on your own.

The Balsams Grand Panorama Golf Club
Route 26, Dixville Notch, NH 03576
603-255-4961
Resort/Public

The Balsams has been home to great golf for nearly 90 years. Generous fairways flanked by deep rough and water on most holes define this grand mountaintop course with plenty of well-placed bunkers and spectacular views. The course and Grand Resort Hotel sit on 15,000 acres, which become a ski haven when you can't golf.

Yardage: 5,069 to 6,804 / 3 sets of tees

Par: 72

Open: May through November

Tee times: Up to 3 days in advance

Green fees: $60 (cart $13 extra per person)

Facility includes: Clubhouse, pro shop, driving range, putting green, 9-hole executive course, restaurant

Packages with Grand Resort.

Bayberry Hills Golf Course
635 West Yarmouth Road, West Yarmouth, MA 02673
508-394-5597
Public

Bayberry is a nice Geoffrey Cornish layout—tight and well wooded with plenty of pines and oaks. Not as tough to get on as some others on the Cape, Bayberry lets you muscle up and fire away—provided you can hit it straight while aiming for large greens on this 7,000+ yard course. Sporting some hills, this is one of the best courses in the area.

Yardage: 5,323 to 7,100 / 4 sets of tees

Par: 72

Open: April through November

Tee times: Up to 4 days in advance, up to 1 month in advance with payment

Green fees: $40 (cart $23 extra)

Facility includes: Clubhouse, pro shop, driving range, 2 putting greens, restaurant, snack bar

Works with area hotels.

Cranberry Valley Golf Course
183 Oak Street, Harwich, MA 02645
508-430-7560
Semi-Private

Large tees lead to large greens on this 25-year-old course that plays through woods, marshlands, and cranberry bogs. (Bring your bog iron.) Well-situated bunkers and sea breezes can play havoc with your shots as you wind your way around numerous doglegs and some water. A couple of long par 3s don't make it any easier on a course that is both tough and forgiving.

Yardage: 5,518 to 6,745 / 4 sets of tees

Par: 72

Open: March through November

Tee times: Up to 2 days in advance, up to 10 days in advance with prepayment check

Green fees: $45 (cart $20 extra)

Facility includes: Clubhouse, pro shop, driving range, chipping area, putting green, snack bar

Farm Neck Golf Club
Farm Neck Way off County Road, Oak Bluffs, MA 02557
508-693-3057
Semi-Private

Sitting on Martha's Vineyard, a 40-minute ferry ride from the mainland, Farm Neck is a beautifully scenic course that requires strategy and good shot-making skills. Carved into the woods on the front nine, the course opens up on the back. Spectacular ocean views, wildflowers, wildlife, six water hazards, and well-placed bunkers define Farm Neck. Since President Clinton played there in 1993, it has been tougher to get on.

Yardage: 6,200 to 6,800 / 3 sets of tees

Par: 72

Open: April through December

Tee times: Up to 2 days in advance

Green fees: Seasonal from $36 to $80 (carts $13.25 extra per person)

Facility includes: Clubhouse, pro shop, driving range, putting green, restaurant

Members only from 8 to 11 a.m.

George Wright Golf Course
420 West Street, Hyde Park, MA 02136
617-361-8313
Public

Within 30 minutes of downtown Boston, this Donald Ross design is a basic public course perfect for when you just want to get out and play before or after business—or take business with you. The not-too-long course is wooded, hilly, and a fairly good test.

Yardage: 5,131 6,500 / 3 sets of tees

Par: 70

Open: Year-round

Tee times: First come for weekdays, call Thursday at 11 a.m. for weekends

Green fees: $21 for Boston residents and $24 for non-residents Monday through Thursday, $24 for residents and $27 for non-residents Friday through Sunday (cart $23 extra)

Facility includes: Clubhouse, pro shop, putting green, snack bar

Maplegate Country Club
160 Maple Street, Bellingham, MA 02019
508-966-4040
Public

A tough course for a scratch golfer, Maplegate is tight and wooded with some water and tough doglegs sending you in both directions with some sharp angles. Smooth, standard-size greens await, but you'll need to hit it accurately to get there. Maplegate is about 45 minutes from Boston.

Yardage: 4,852 to 6,815 / 3 sets of tees

Par: 72

Open: Year-round

Tee times: Up to 6 days in advance

Green fees: $36 weekdays, $43 weekends (cart $13 extra per person)

Facility includes: Clubhouse, pro shop, driving range, putting green, snack bar

Mt. Snow Golf Club
Country Club Road, West Dover, VT 05356
800-451-4211
Resort

A beautiful course, Mt. Snow has rolling to hilly terrain with plenty of well-placed, white sand traps and a few water

(Mt. Snow Golf Club cont'd)

hazards. Fairways are open, but the hazards will make you plan your shots carefully toward undulating greens that are flanked by ponds and bunkers. Just over an hour from Albany, this popular New England resort offers golf (and skiing) in a relaxed low-key environment with plenty of wildlife, including birds and foxes that call the course home.

Yardage: 5,824 to 6,819 / 3 sets of tees

Par: 74/72

Open: May through October

Tee times: Up to 3 days in advance

Green fees: $63, including cart

Facility includes: Clubhouse, pro shop, driving range, putting green, golf school, restaurant

Packages with resort and with Snow Lake Lodge and Grand Summit Resort Hotel.

New England Country Club
180 Paine Street, Bellingham, MA 02019
508-883-2300
Public

Just 35 miles from Boston sits this public, country-club–style course that features target golf through trees, around hazards (some hidden), and over marshlands. The course is not particularly long but forces you to be accurate and use strategy.

Yardage: 4,908 to 6,500 / 4 sets of tees

Par: 71

Open: March through November

Tee times: Up to 5 days in advance, Wednesdays for the weekend

Green fees: $45 weekdays, $50 Fridays, $60 weekends, including cart

Facility includes: Clubhouse, pro shop, driving range, putting green, restaurant

Portsmouth Country Club
1 Country Club Lane, Greenland, NH 03840
603-436-9719
Semi-Private

Sitting on a peninsula, this is a links-style course that can become the ultimate test when the winds and rain kick up. As you wind your way along the shoreline, you'll be challenged to stay away from the marshlands, sand traps, and the water (which you can see from everywhere). The relatively flat Robert Trent Jones course is the longest in the state and sits just 10 minutes from Portsmouth.

Yardage: 5,400 to 7,050 / 3 sets of tees

Par: 78/72

Open: Mid April through November

Tee times: Up to 1 day in advance

Green fees: $60 (cart $25 extra)

Facility includes: Clubhouse, pro shop, driving range, putting green, restaurant

Rutland Country Club
North Grove Street, Rutland, VT 05701
802-773-3254
Semi-Private

Built in 1901, Rutland is a relatively short course with some elevation changes that will test your iron and putting game (big time). The tough greens, protected by 45 traps, are well contoured, undulating, sloping, or protected by some type of hazard. The old course is one of the top-rated courses in the state and sits 30 miles from Manchester.

Yardage: 5,368 to 6,134 / 4 sets of tees

Par: 70

Open: April through October

Tee times: Up to 2 days in advance

(Rutland Country Club cont'd)

Green fees: $70, including cart

Facility includes: Clubhouse, pro shop, driving net, putting green, restaurant

---

The Sheridan Colonial Hotel and Golf Club
1 Audubon Road, Lynnfield, MA 01940
781-245-9300
Public

From 1929, this course is championship caliber with a typical New England ambiance. Some hills, some water, a fair amount of trees, and a few elevation changes lead to bent-grass greens. Only 15 minutes from Boston, this is one of the closest courses that can provide a solid round of play.

Yardage: 5,280 to 6,565 / 3 sets of tees

Par: 72/70

Open: Mid March through November

Tee times: Up to 3 days in advance

Green fees: $50 to $60, including cart

Facility includes: Clubhouse, pro shop, driving range, putting range

Packages with Sheridan.

Sugarloaf Golf Club
RR #1 P.O. Box 5000, Carrabassett Valley, ME 04947
207-237-6806
Resort

Arguably the best course in the state of Maine, Sugarloaf has 18 distinct holes with each fairway carved out of the woods and no two fairways in view of each other. The tree-lined mountain course sports some significant elevation changes and magnificent fall scenery.

Yardage: 5,376 to 6,924 / 4 sets of tees

Par: 72

Open: April through September

Tee times: Up to 14 days in advance

Green fees: $66 to $95, including cart

Facility includes: Clubhouse, pro shop, driving range, chipping area, putting green

Packages with first class resort.

Taconic Golf Club
Meacham Street, Williamstown, MA 01267
413-458-3997
Semi-Private

Just over 100 years old, the Taconic Golf Club has tree-lined fairways and great scenery. Smack dab in the middle of the Berkshire Mountains, Taconic has narrow landing areas on well-maintained fairways leading to bent-grass greens. The highly ranked old course is only 10 minutes from Vermont and 45 minutes from Albany.

Yardage: 5,202 to 6,640 / 4 sets of tees

Par: 71

Open: Mid April through November

Tee times: Up to 7 days in advance

Green fees: $125, including cart

Facility includes: Clubhouse, pro shop, driving range (in the spring), putting green, chipping and sand practice areas, restaurant

Open for public play Tuesday through Friday only.

Chicago

Cincinnati

Cleveland

Chicago

One of the richest golfing areas in the country, Chicago is a major market with a number of championship-level courses. Seven area clubs have hosted U.S. Opens, and numerous other top tournaments have been played in and around the Windy City. With the exception of the three winter months, golf is extremely popular and courses are busy.

Area courses run the gamut from traditional Midwestern with plenty of trees to some newer links-style settings. For travelers, a dozen or more solid facilities are within an hour of either O'Hare airport or downtown Chicago. Get your foursome together ahead of time if possible and book in advance. Because of the popularity of the game, Chicago courses have a 24- or 48-hour cancellation policy. Most hotels will arrange for transportation if you don't have a car. You might also pick up one of two area golf magazines, *Chicago District Golfer* or *Chicagoland Golf*, both of which give you insight into the courses of Chicago.

Cantigny Golf
27 West 270 Mack Road, Wheaton, IL 60187
630-668-8463
Public

A playable public course less than an hour from downtown Chicago, Cantigny features three great nines that offer you three combinations for your round of 18. True to their names: The Hillside is hilly, the Lakeside features water, and the Woodside plays through tree-lined fairways (and is also the most difficult of the three). Well-maintained fast greens are found on all three nines.

Yardage: Woodside, 2,735 to 3,455; Lakeside, 2,686 to 3,374; Hillside, 2,497 to 3,338 / 3 sets of tees each

Par: 72

Open: April through October (closed on Mondays)

Tee times: Up to 7 days in advance

Green fees: 18 holes $70 or $85, including cart or caddie (plus tip)

Facility includes: Clubhouse, pro shop, driving range, chipping area, putting green, restaurant

Cog Hill Golf Club
12294 Archer Avenue, Lemont, IL 60439
630-257-5872
Public

Perhaps the best-known facility in the Chicago area, Cog Hill sports four 18-hole courses. Numbers 1 and 3 are similar layouts in old Midwestern style with plenty of trees and water coming into play on nearly half the holes. Number 2 is a popular wooded ravine course. It's scenic and challenging but has some easier holes than Number 4, which, although built on similar terrain, is arguably the toughest in Chicago. An annual stop on the PGA tour, Number 4 has been named the

Dubsdread and features oak-lined fairways, undulating greens, and a signature hole with a four-tiered green. Like Wrigley field, it's a must for Windy City visitors who play golf.

Yardage: #1, 5,594 to 6,329; #2, 5,564 to 6,268; #3, 5,321 to 6,437; #4, 5,889 to 6,940 / 3 sets of tees each

Par: #1, 71; all others 72

Open: March 15 to October 1

Tee times: Up to 6 days in advance on #1 and #3, up to 90 days in advance on #2 and #4

Green fees: #1, #2, and #3 from $30 and $40, $95 on #4 (carts $28 extra for 2 riders, $18 extra for 1)

Facility includes: Clubhouse, pro shop, driving range, putting green, sand and chipping practice areas, restaurant

George W. Dunne National Golf Course
16310 Central Avenue, Oak Forest, IL 60452
708-429-6886
Public

Bent-grass fairways and greens with 64 sand traps and water on nearly half the holes describe this long, tree-lined Midwestern course. A 40-minute ride from the Loop, Dunne National is a highly regarded course and, through word of mouth, has become popular with all levels of players.

Yardage: 5,535 to 7,170 / 4 sets of tees

Par: 72

Open: April through November

Tee times: Up to 7 days in advance

Green fees: $35 weekdays, $40 weekends (carts $20 extra)

Facility includes: Clubhouse, pro shop, driving range, two putting greens, snack bar

Harborside International Golf Center
11001 South Doty Avenue, Chicago, IL 60628
312-782-7837
Public

Two popular new public courses (Port and Starboard) sit on a 450-acre landfill in the city itself. Both links-style courses feature plenty of water, numerous sand bunkers, and well-contoured greens in a wide-open, somewhat windy setting that overlooks the harbor.

Yardage: Port, 5,164 to 7,164; Starboard, 5,110 to 7,166 / 4 sets of tees each

Par: 72

Open: March through November

Tee times: Up to 14 days in advance

Green fees: $65 weekdays, $75 weekends, including cart

Facility includes: Clubhouse, pro shop, driving range, putting greens, golf academy, restaurant

Kemper Lakes Golf Course
Old McHenery Road, Long Grove, IL 60049
847-320-3450
Public

A popular course only 45 minutes from the Loop, Kemper sees a number of major tournaments and a tremendous amount of corporate play. The long course is complete with water on nearly half the holes, plus a lot of trees and sand. Some hills come into play on the back nine, whereas the greens are well maintained and on the fast side throughout. Kemper is a solid test for all player levels and will have you using all the clubs in your bag.

Yardage: 5,638 to 7,217 / 4 sets of tees

Par: 72

Open: April through November

Tee times: Up to 7 days in advance, 48-hour cancellation policy

Green fees: $120, including cart

Facility includes: Clubhouse, pro shop, driving range, putting green, restaurant with dining room and banquet facilities

---

Klein Creek Golf Club
1 North 333 Pleasant Hill Road, Winfield, IL 60190
630-690-0101
Public

A tight target golf course designed for accurate hitters, Klien features over 160 traps and plenty of water holes to make life more difficult. About 30 minutes from Chicago, the Creek course is a fairly new, scenic, public facility in excellent condition and very popular with the corporate crowd.

Yardage: 4,909 to 6,701 / 4 sets of tees

Par: 72

Open: Year-round

Tee times: Up to 14 days in advance

Green fees: $63 weekdays, $73 weekends, including cart

Facility includes: Clubhouse, pro shop, putting green, restaurants

---

Pine Meadow Golf Club
1 Pine Meadow Lane, Mundline, IL 60060
847-566-4653
Public

Pine Meadow is a tough, long course that even has 200-yard par 3s from the back tees. Wide fairways offer plenty of room, but you'd better stay on them; there is extremely thick rough sitting out of bounds. A lot of water comes into play on the back nine as you head to large, undulating greens that are

(Pine Meadow Golf Club cont'd)

fast. Pine Meadows draws a lot of visitors from Chicago, just an hour away.

Yardage: 5,023 to 7,141 / 5 sets of tees

Par: 71/72

Open: April through October

Tee times: Up to 120 days in advance for foursomes, up to 2 days in advance for less than 4 (48-hour cancellation policy for foursomes)

Green fees: $63 (cart $28 extra per person), $77 per person with shared cart

Facility includes: Clubhouse, pro shop, driving range, practice range, putting, casual restaurant

Prairie Landing Golf Course
2325 Longest Drive, West Chicago, IL 61086
630-208-7600
Public

Prairie Landing serves up a links-style front nine with some trees on the back nine. Tall grass surrounding clean-cut fairways, prairie lands, numerous sand bunkers, and a tough finishing hole by a pond characterize this challenging course, which is about 40 minutes from downtown.

Yardage: 4,859 to 6,862 / 4 sets of tees

Par: 72

Open: April through October

Tee times: Up to 14 days in advance for foursomes; otherwise, up to 2 days in advance

Green fees: $82, including cart

Facility includes: Pro shop, driving range, practice holes, restaurant

Ruffled Feathers Golf Club
1 Pete Dye Drive, Lemont, IL 60439
630-257-1000
Public

Water, sand, and trees will ruffle your feathers on this tough, tight Pete Dye course complete with fast greens (once you get to them). A busy corporate course, Ruffled Feathers is only 30 minutes from Chicago but has anything but an urban look to it with nearby wildlife.

Yardage: 5,273 to 6,878 / 5 sets of tees

Par: 72

Open: Late March through November

Tee times: Up to 14 days in advance, 48-hour cancellation policy

Green fees: $60 to $110 depending on time of day, including cart

Facility includes: Clubhouse, pro shop, driving range, putting green, restaurant and banquet facilities

Seven Bridges Golf Course
One Mulligan Drive, Woodridge, IL 60517
630-964-7777
Public

Seven Bridges offers a lot of water on the front nine leading to a dryer, yet difficult back nine. Medium quick, large, undulating greens await you once you maneuver around or through about 160 bunkers on this mature, well-kept, long course, just over 30 minutes from the Loop.

Yardage: 5,263 to 7,103 / 4 sets of tees

Par: 72

Open: Mid March through mid November

Tee times: Up to 14 days in advance for foursome; otherwise, up to 7 days in advance, 24-hour cancellation policy

(Seven Bridges Golf Course cont'd)

Green fees: $89, including cart

Facility includes: Clubhouse, pro shop, driving range, putting green

---

WeaverRidge Golf Club
5100 WeaverRidge Boulevard, Peoria, IL 61615
309-691-3344
Public

If you venture a couple of hours from Chicago into Peoria or you have business in Central Illinois, you might want to check out this beautiful course with rolling hills, tree-lined fairways, and dramatic elevation changes. One hole has a 120-foot drop from the tee area to the fairway. It's a good reason to get out of town for a day.

Yardage: 5,046 to 7,030 / 5 sets of tees

Par: 72

Open: Year-round

Tee time: Up to 14 days in advance

Green fees: $48 Monday through Wednesday, $58 Thursday through Sunday (carts $10 extra per person)

Facility includes: Clubhouse, pro shop, driving range, chipping, area, putting green, computerized in-cart monitor (reads course) $5 extra per person

Hotel packages available in Peoria.

Cincinnati

Cincinnati is somewhat unique for the eastern part of the country in that many area courses are within the city boundaries. Courses have been designed by Arthur Hill, Jack Nicholas, and several other top names. Within 15 minutes from downtown hotels, you can hit away on any of several first-rate layouts that vary in style and difficulty. With the exception of January and February, golf is played almost year-round, weather permitting. The terrain favors hilly courses, and most offer their share of trees indigenous to the area.

Just outside the city, you can play Shaker Run, which is probably the best known course in the area. A popular public facility that even sells clothing with its logo, Shaker Run is owned by a parent company that has opened Beaver Creek and Walden Pond. You can find packages to play the three courses, and affiliations have been set up with local hotels. Most of the area hotels work with the various courses to arrange tee times. *Tri-State Golf Magazine*, 888-801-GOLF, is worth picking up to read more about golf in Cincinnati.

Beaver Creek Golf Club
2800 New Germany Road, Beaver Creek, OH 45324
937-320-0742
Public

Rolling terrain and a meandering creek create a relaxed atmosphere at this Fuzzy Zoeller signature course, an hour from downtown. The layout offers a nice mix with some wide-open holes and others winding through the trees.

Yardage: 5,101 to 7,030 / 4 sets of tees

Par: 72

Open: Year-round

Tee times: Up to 7 days in advance

Green fees: Seasonal from $30 to $55, including cart

Facility includes: Clubhouse, pro shop, driving range, chipping area, putting green, restaurant and banquet facilities, snack bar

Three-course membership plan with Shaker Run and Walden Pond and packages with nearby Springfield Inn.

Blue Ash Golf Course
4040 Cooper Road, Cincinnati, OH 45242
513-745-8577
Public

Blue Ash is one of the highest rated public facilities in the area. Easy to get to, this beautiful course is long, tight, and hilly with large undulating greens. Blue Ash will test all aspects of your game, but you must be persistent in trying to get on because this course is very popular.

Yardage: 5,125 to 6,659 / 4 sets of tees

Par: 72

Open: Year-round

Tee time: Up to 5 days in advance

Green fees: $24 walking, $35 with cart

Facility includes: Clubhouse, pro shop, putting green, restaurant

Downtown hotels will help you set up tee times.

Golf Center at Kings Island
6042 Fairway Drive, Mason, OH 45040
513-398-7700
Public

Formerly a Jack Nicholas course, the Golf Center now features three 9-hole designs that provide rolling fairways, high rough, and water on some tough par 3s. Any configuration will provide a good round. There is also an executive par 3 Bruin course on the premises.

Yardage: 5,176 to 6,795 depending on configuration / 4 sets of tees

Par: 71

Open: Year-round

Tee time: Up to 7 days in advance

Green fees: $45 Monday through Thursday, $55 Friday, $65 weekend, including cart

Facility includes: Clubhouse, pro shop, driving range, chipping area, putting green, restaurant

---

Glenview Golf Course
10965 Springfield Pike, Cincinnati, OH 45246
513-651-4653 tee times
513-771-1747 pro shop
Public

A 25-year-old popular course, Glenview offers a somewhat difficult layout with many trees and bent-grass greens on two distinct nines. The easily accessible, in-city course is well maintained, considering the amount of play.

Yardage: 5,305 to 6,843 / 4 sets of tees

Par: 72

Open: Year-round

Tee times: Up to 5 days in advance with automated tee service, or call pro shop

Green fees: $20 (cart $20 extra)

Facility includes: Historic clubhouse, pro shop, driving range, putting green

---

Indian Valley Golf Course
3950 Newtown Road, Cincinnati, OH 45244
513-561-9491
Public

A flat, not very long course, the back nine at Indian Valley is somewhat tighter than the front. Sand traps and some bunkers prevail, but otherwise, the layout is a relatively risk-free course that lets you build confidence in your game. The greens are excellent, fast, and of the bent-grass variety.

(Indian Valley Golf Course cont'd)

Yardage: 4,494 to 6,007 / 3 sets of tees

Par: 70

Open: Year-round

Tee time: Up to 14 days in advance

Green fees: $17.75 walking, $20.50 riding

Facility includes: Clubhouse, pro shop, putting green, restaurant

---

Lassing Pointe Golf Club
2266 Double Eagle Drive, Union, KY 41091
606-384-2266
Public

One of the premier public courses in the state of Kentucky, Lassing Pointe is a chip shot from Cincinnati, about 15 minutes away. The five-year-old course is the target golf variety, featuring bent grass from tees to large undulating greens. The well-maintained facility is scenic and has a character all its own.

Yardage: 5,153 to 6,724 / 4 sets of tees

Par: 71

Open: April through November (closed Mondays)

Tee times: Up to 7 days in advance for weekdays, from the prior Thursday for weekends

Green fees: $26 walking, $36 riding

Facility includes: Clubhouse, pro shop, driving range, 2 putting greens, cafeteria

---

Pebble Creek Country Club
9799 Prechtel Road, Cincinnati, OH 45252
513-385-4442
Public

No, it's not up to par with Pebble Beach in Monterey, but Pebble Creek is a lot cheaper. This fun course combines target golf with a number of hills. Some tough par 5s, plenty of trees, bent-grass tees throughout, and a par 3 finishing hole with an island green make for a diverse round of golf.

Yardage: 4,805 to 6,316 / 3 sets of tees

Par: 71

Open: Year-round

Tee times: Up to 4 days in advance

Green fees: $23 weekdays, $28 weekends (cart $12 extra per person)

Facility includes: Clubhouse, pro shop, putting green

Reeves Golf Course
4747 Playfield Land, Cincinnati, OH 45226
513-321-2740
Public

This is a links-style, accessible city course that, if not too crowded, will provide a basic no-frills round of golf in a friendly low-key atmosphere. The course is relatively flat and wide open and good for newer players.

Yardage: 5,747 to 6,033 / 2 sets of tees

Par: 74/70

Open: Year-round

Tee times: Call within 24 hours

Green fees: $17.50 walking, $28 riding

Facility includes: Clubhouse, pro shop, driving range, putting green, par 3 course, restaurant

---

Shaker Run Golf Course
4361 Greentree Road, Lebanon, OH 45036
513-727-0007
Public

One of the best-known, highest-rated courses in the state, Shaker Run is worth a short jaunt from Cincinnati. Only 40

(Shaker Run Golf Course cont'd)

minutes away, Shaker Run offers a long, tight layout complete with many trees, some water, fast, tricky greens, and great scenic views. If all that isn't enough, they're adding nine new holes in spring 1999.

Yardage: 6,385 to 6,965 / 4 sets of tees

Par: 72

Open: Year-round

Tee times: Up to 7 days in advance or guaranteed any time for $10 per person extra

Green fees: Seasonal from $39 to $75, including cart

Facility includes: Clubhouse, pro shop, driving range, 2 putting greens, grill

Coupon books available at course; packages with Manchester Inn in Middletown, Hamiltonian in Hamilton and a three-course corporate membership are available.

Sharon Woods Golf Course
11350 Swing Road, Cincinnati, OH 45241
513-769-4325
Public

A 70-year-old country-style course with natural terrain, this long, tight layout is a good test for all golfers—especially those who appreciate hills and elevation changes. Tough par 3s and long par 4s make this a demanding layout. Fifteen minutes from the heart of the city, the suburban course is popular during the spring and summer.

Yardage: 5,288 to 6,652 / 3 sets of tees

Par: 70

Open: March through December

Tee times: Up to 5 days in advance

Green fees: $18.50 walking, $29.50 riding

Facility includes: Clubhouse, pro shop, practice greens, restaurant

Vineyard Golf Course
600 Nordyke Road, Cincinnati, OH 45255
513-474-3007
Public

One of the premiere courses in the area, Vineyard is easily accessible from anywhere in the city and offers a first-rate round of golf—plus amenities and excellent service. Soft rolling terrain, bent-grass fairways and greens, and 46 white-sand bunkers characterize this country-club–style, well-maintained public course. Bring your best putting game.

Yardage: 4,747 to 6,789 / 3 sets of tees

Par: 71

Open: Mid March through November

Tee times: Up to 5 days in advance, beginning at 6 p.m.

Green fees: $25.50 walking, $37 riding

Facility includes: Clubhouse, pro shop, 2 putting greens, restaurant

Works with downtown and nearby hotels.

Walden Ponds Golf Club
6090 Golf Club Lane, Indian Springs, OH 45011
513-785-2999
Public

A new links-style course, Walden Ponds is built on an old estate, using the estate itself (from 1830) as a clubhouse and the carriage house as a pro shop. The picturesque layout includes bent-grass tees, fairways, and greens, 85 bunkers, and 9 ponds. Only 40 minutes from downtown, the third of the Shaker Company trio of courses, Walden is worth the ride.

Yardage: 4,885 to 7,001 / 4 sets of tees

Par: 72

Open: Year-round

Tee times: Up to 7 days in advance

(Waldon Ponds Golf Club cont'd)

Green fees: $45 Monday through Thursday, $55 Friday through Sunday, including cart

Facility includes: Clubhouse, pro shop, driving range, putting green, golf academy, grill

Offers a three-course corporate membership package with Shaker Run and Beaver Creek, plus hotel packages with Manchester Inn and the Hamiltonian.

Cleveland

Six metro courses occupy the city itself, and many more old courses exist within an hour of downtown Cleveland. Local hotels can help with neighboring courses; Metro Golf, 440-232-2722, can help with details on city courses. Most area courses are not very expensive; many run under $50 with cart, although many layouts are walkable.

Courses vary in style, and many blend nicely with their natural surroundings, such as Fowler's Mill, which is a Certified Audubon Cooperative Sanctuary Golf Course, designated for its environmental efforts. Trees, hills, lakes, and other area topography typifies most traditional area courses. Players can be found hitting away nine months out of the year, unless a mild winter allows for a full year of golf.

Boston Hills Country Club
105 East Hines Hill Road, Hudson, OH 44236
330-656-2438
Public

A fun, short layout, Boston Hills is a pleasant open course with some water, a number of traps, and tiny greens that will test your chipping game. The 75-year-old walkable layout is 45 minutes from downtown Cleveland.

Yardage: 4,987 to 6,167 / 4 sets of tees

Par: 71

Open: Year-round

Tee times: Up to 7 days in advance

Green fees: $19 weekdays, $24 weekends (carts $10 extra per person)

Facility includes: Clubhouse, pro shop, driving range, putting green, grill

Discounts from Holiday Inn in Hudson.

Brandywine Country Club
5555 Peninsula Road, Peninsula, OH 44264
216-657-2525
Public

The front nine is wide open despite a host of trees indigenous to the region. The back nine is much tighter with hills coming into play. The course is 45 minutes from Cleveland, just a few minutes from Akron, and sees plenty of activity from both cities.

Yardage: 5,625 to 6,481 / 3 sets of tees

Par: 72

Open: Year-round

Tee times: Up to 14 days in advance

Green fees: $20 walking and $26 riding on weekdays, $25 walking and $36 riding on weekends

Facility includes: Clubhouse, pro shop, putting green, snack bar

Works with area hotels.

Briarwood Golf Course
2737 Edgerton Road, Broadview Heights, OH 44147
440-237-5271
Public

Three 9-hole courses make up Briarwood. They offer a nice variety of holes with both tight and open fairways, some

(Briarwood Golf Course cont'd)

hills, a little water on each nine, and bent-grass greens on all three. The busy course sees a lot of visitors because it is 40 minutes from downtown and 30 minutes from the airport.

Yardage: 5,790 to 6,995 / 3 sets of tees

Par: 72/71

Open: April through December

Tee times: Up to 7 days in advance for foursomes

Green fees: $20 weekdays, $25 weekends (carts $22 extra)

Facility includes: Clubhouse, pro shop, driving range, snack bar

Talk to downtown and airport hotels for tee times.

Fowler's Mill Golf Course
13095 Rockhaven Road, Chesterland, OH 44026
440-729-7569
Public

A beautiful stream flows through Fowler's Mill, which takes up a small portion of a 400-acre property that enhances nature, with deer and other wildlife making their home in the thick grass that surrounds the tough Pete Dye course. Three 9-hole layouts, the Lake, River, and Maple courses, provide interesting holes with creeks splitting fairways in two, a lake running alongside, and well-placed bunkers making sure you stay on the fairway you choose. As expected, there is more water present on and around the Lake and River courses, whereas the Maple nine is tighter with more trees and smaller greens. Fowler's is 35 miles north of Cleveland.

Yardage: Lake 3,033 to 3,606; River 2,917 to 3,396; Maple 2,880 to 2,989 / 3 sets of tees

Par: Lake and River 36; Maple 35

Open: Year-round

Tee time: Up to 14 days in advance

Green fees: $25 to $47 weekdays (depending on time of day), $57 Friday through Sunday, including cart

Facility includes: Clubhouse, pro shop, driving range, putting green, grill and banquet facility

---

Sawmill Creek Golf and Racquet Club
2401 Cleveland Road, West Huron, OH 44839
419-433-3789
Resort/Public

A well-maintained Carolina-esque layout, Sawmill sports plenty of pines on a tight layout with fast, spacious, undulating greens. Surrounded on three sides by water, including Lake Erie, a nature preserve, and a creek, 14 of 18 holes play over or around the water. Difficult par 3s round out the experience on this lodge course that is just over an hour west of Cleveland.

Yardage: 5,124 to 6,702 / 4 sets of tees

Par: 71

Open: Mid April through October

Tee times: Up to 3 days in advance; resort guests, when making room reservations

Green fees: $54 weekdays, $58 weekends (cart $15 extra per person)

Facility includes: Clubhouse, pro shop, chipping area, putting green, restaurant, snack bar

Lodge offers golf packages.

Sleepy Hollow Golf Course
9445 Brecksville Road, Brecksville, OH 44141
216-526-4285
Public

A punitive course that works the old risk and reward system to a "tee," forcing you to play a solid mental as well as

(Sleepy Hollow Golf Course cont'd)

physical game. This tough course is tight with peaks and valleys, making it challenging to low handicappers. Greens are tricky once you get there. A short ride south from Cleveland, Sleepy Hollow sees a lot of traffic but is kept in good condition as part of the Cleveland area Metro Park Course system.

Yardage: 5,715 to 6,630 / 3 sets of tees

Par: 73/71

Open: March through December

Tee times: Up to 5 days in advance

Green fees: $21 weekdays, $23 weekends (cart $10 extra per person)

Facility includes: Clubhouse, driving range, putting green, snack bar

Works with area hotels.

Dallas/Ft. Worth

Denver

Dallas/Ft. Worth

The rolling plain terrain of the Dallas area allows for some exciting courses with elevation changes on tree-lined courses. The best time to play in the area is usually the spring and the fall when the weather is perfect for golf. Half a dozen city courses in the Dallas/Ft. Worth area are in excellent shape and the neighboring areas sport sprawling resort courses.

You can find *North Texas Golfer Magazine* and golf city maps that contain local information at hotels, local bookstores, and pro shops or by calling 713-464-0308.

Area hotels work with courses to help book reservations, and resorts offer packages at good rates (in comparison to some other markets).

The Cliffs Golf Club
HC51, Box 19, Graford, TX 76449
888-843-2543
Resort/Public

Ranked one of the top 10 toughest courses in Texas, this resort layout is both a beauty and a beast. The course sits atop a cliff looking down on Possum Kingdom Lake. There are a lot of cliffs and ravines and many blind shots. Wear high boots because you might encounter rattlesnakes. The Cliffs is an hour and a half outside of Ft. Worth.

Yardage: 4,876 to 6,808 / 4 sets of tees

Par: 71

Open: Year-round (closed Tuesdays)

Tee times: Up to 7 days in advance, up to 1 month in advance with resort reservation

Green fees: $42 Monday through Thursday, $60 Friday, $75 Saturday and Sunday

Facility includes: Clubhouse, pro shop, driving range, chipping area, putting green, restaurants, snack bar, conference center, marina

Packages available with the Inn at the Cliffs.

Firewheel Golf Park
600 West Blackburn Road, Garland, TX 75044
972-205-2795
Public

Firewheel offers two courses only 10 miles from downtown Dallas. The Lake course is very challenging, requiring precise shots, with a lot of water and tight fairways full of sand traps. The Old course is a more traditional, longer course with wide-open fairways.

Yardage: Lake, 5,200 to 6,600; Old, 5,600 to 7,054 / 4 sets of tees each

Par: Lake, 71; Old, 72

Open: Year-round

Tee times: Thursday 8 a.m. for the next 7 days

Green fees: $18 Monday through Thursday, $26 Friday through Sunday (cart $10 extra per person)

Facility includes: Clubhouse, pro shop, driving areas, chipping area, putting green, restaurant

---

Garden Valley Golf Resort
22049 FM Road 1995, Lindale, TX 75771
903-882-6107
800-443-8577 tee times
Resort/Public

The Garden Resort offers two courses: the newer Dogwood and the Hummingbird. The Dogwood is a championship-quality course with bent-grass greens. It's tree-lined with some water holes and tough rough areas. The fairways are medium length and difficult on this beautiful course, which is full of flowers and a delight to the eye. The Hummingbird is the older of the two and is easier to play. This is also a tree-lined design, shorter and attractive, but not as stunning as its sister course.

Yardage: Dogwood, 5,532 to 6,753; Hummingbird, 5,131 to 6,446 / 3 sets of tees each

Par: Dogwood, 72; Hummingbird, 71

Open: Year-round

Tee times: Up to 60 days in advance

Green fees: Dogwood, $56 Monday through Thursday, $64 Friday through Sunday; Hummingbird $20 Monday through Thursday, $25 Friday through Sunday, including cart

Facility includes: Clubhouse, pro shop, driving range, putting green, bar and grill, conference banquet hall, restaurant

Packages with local hotels in Tyler.

Pecan Valley Golf Course
6400 Pecan Drive, Ft. Worth, TX 76132
817-249-1845
Public

Two courses, the Hills and the River, make up Pecan Valley. The names are very representative because the Hills features hilly, wide-open fairways with sparse landscaping and some bunkers to make it interesting. The River course offers tree-lined fairways with a river running through two holes and lakes on several others. The municipal layouts are accessible, right in Ft. Worth.

Yardage: Hills, 5,275 to 6,777; River, 5,419 to 6,562 / 3 sets of tees each

Par: Hills, 72; River, 71

Open: Year-round

Tee times: Up to 7 days in advance if in the computer system, 5 days in advance if not

Green fees: Hills, $12 weekdays, $16 weekends; River, $15 weekdays, $20 weekends (carts $19.50 extra each course)

Facility includes: Clubhouse, pro shop, driving range, chipping area, putting green, snack bar

Tanglewood Resort
Highway 120 North, Pottsboro, TX 75076
903-786-4140
800-833-6569
Resort

This beautiful and scenic resort offers a terrific golfing experience. The course has rolling hills with some tree-lined fairways en route to well-manicured greens. Water comes into play on five holes. For resort guests only (or members), Tanglewood is just over an hour from Dallas.

Yardage: 5,000 to 7,000 / 4 sets of tees

Par: 72

Open: Year-round

Tee times: Up to 4 weeks in advance

Green fees: $44 weekdays, $55 weekends, including cart

Facility includes: Clubhouse, pro shop, driving range, putting green, restaurant

Packages with resort.

Denver

You can find a lot of first-rate scenic and challenging courses in and around Denver. Styles vary, and in some cases, the elevation will let you surprise yourself with your driving prowess. Downtown hotels will help you get onto the city courses, or you can call 303-794-4000 to reserve three days ahead with a $10 reservation card. Resident cards are popular for city players, offering advance tee time benefits. When in the area, you might pick up *Colorado Golf Magazine* or call them at 303-688-8262.

Although the courses in Denver are fun and excellent for those without the time to venture out of the immediate area, within an hour's drive are many more spectacular courses in all directions from the city. Several top resorts offer golf packages and other amenities for business travel, meetings, or vacationers. The high season for golf is May through September, and December through February are better for skiing, although most courses stay open if the ground remains dry.

Arrowhead Golf Course
10850 West Sundown Trail, Littleton, CO 80125
303-973-9614
Resort/Public

Spectacular views and wildlife may distract you on this course (20 minutes from downtown Denver), which has been described as topographically astonishing. The tough mountain

(Arrowhead Golf Course cont'd)

layout plays through tree-lined and rock-lined fairways. Thick rough, many traps, some water, and fast, medium-sized greens further describe the layout. Bring your best game and your camera.

Yardage: 5,465 to 6,662 / 3 sets of tees

Par: 72/70

Open: March through November

Tee times: Up to 7 days in advance, up to 14 days in advance with $10 reservation card, 48-hour cancellation policy

Green fees: Seasonal from $65 to $95, including cart

Facility includes: Clubhouse, pro shop, driving range, putting green, restaurant

---

Broadmoor Golf Club
1 Pourtales Drive, Colorado Springs, CO 80906
800-634-7711
Resort

An hour south of Denver, Broadmoor offers three excellent 18-hole courses for guests of the five-star resort. The 80-year-old East course is a long, open, and flat course with water and tricky greens. The West course starts open and then plays tightly through the foothills on the back nine. The newer Mountains course is 1,000 feet higher in elevation and is a shorter but tougher course, offering target golf through a ravine. Don't slice or hook on this one. The landmark 700-room resort offers everything from skeet shooting to hot air ballooning.

Yardage: East, 5,913 to 7,091; West, 5,455 to 6,832; Mountain, 5,577 to 6,781 / 3 sets of tees each

Par: East, 72; West, 73/72; Mountain, 72/70

Open: Year-round

Tee times: Up to 60 days in advance (resort guests only)

Green fees: $85 to $130, including cart

Facility includes: Clubhouse with spa, pro shop, 2 driving ranges, putting green, restaurant, snack bar

Resort golf packages.

Fox Hollow at Lakewood
13410 Morrison Road, Lakewood, CO 80228
303-986-7888
Public

Fox Hollow is home to three 9-hole courses only 15 minutes west of downtown Denver. The Canyon nine has water on several holes, tall native grass providing tough rough, and a fifth hole that plays over the canyon. The Meadows course is flat with plenty of water coming into play, whereas the Links is true to its name, featuring mounds, pot bunkers, and rolling hills en route to large, well-bunkered greens.

Yardage: 5,203 to 7,030, depending on configuration / 5 sets of tees

Par: 71/72

Open: Year-round

Tee times: Up to 6 days in advance

Green fees: $33 walking, $45 riding

Facility includes: Clubhouse, pro shop, driving range, putting green, restaurant

Hyland Hills Golf Course
9650 North Sheridan Boulevard, Westminster, CO 80030
303-428-6526
Public

Only 45 minutes from downtown Denver, this links-style layout is long with plenty of water, including some trees and hills on the back nine. The extremely popular course requires on-course playing strategy and tenacious off-course strategy to get on.

(Hyland Hills Golf Course cont'd)

Yardage: 5,654 to 7,029 / 4 sets of tees

Par: 73/72

Open: Year-round

Tee times: Prior day Monday through Friday, prior Wednesday for Saturday, prior Friday for Sunday ($25 reservation card offered for preferred tee times)

Green fees: $23 (cart $20 extra)

Facility includes: Clubhouse, pro shop, driving range, chipping area, sand practice area, putting green, 9-hole par 3 course, restaurant

---

Indian Tree Golf Club
7555 Wadsworth Boulevard, Arvada, CO 80005
303-423-3450
Public

A hilly course, Indian Tree is a walkable layout with a number of placed bunkers per hole and water on seven holes. You'll need some luck on the 13th hole with two lakes and a waterfall to contend with. Indian Tree sits only 15 minutes from the city.

Yardage: 5,850 to 6,742 / 3 sets of tees

Par: 75/70

Open: Year-round

Tee times: Up to 2 days in advance, up to 3 days in advance with $10 reservation card

Green fees: $20 (cart $20 extra)

Facility includes: Clubhouse, pro shop, driving range, putting green, par 3 course, restaurant

Inverness Golf Course
20 Inverness Drive West, Englewood, CO 80112
303-790-4341
Resort

A highly rated resort facility, Inverness offers guests a traditional tree-lined, hilly course that plays in and out of the valley and features water on 12 holes. Only three miles from Denver, the resort provides business and vacation travelers luxury, first-rate golf and easy access to city locations and to the airport.

Yardage: 5,681 to 6,948 / 3 sets of tees

Par: 70

Open: Year-round

Tee times: When making room reservation

Green fees: $90 weekdays, $100 weekends, including cart

Facility includes: Clubhouse, pro shop, driving range, putting green, restaurants

Resort packages available.

Keystone Ranch Golf Course
Keystone Ranch, Dylan, CO 90435
800-354-4386
Resort

This tough mountain course is perfect for golfers who enjoy hiking. Some dramatic elevation changes highlight Keystone as it plays through the river valley and through a forest. Blue grass tees and fairways lead to bent-grass greens on this resort course, which is only 90 minutes from downtown Denver.

Yardage: 5,720 to 7,090 / 3 sets of tees

Par: 72

Open: Year-round

Tee times: Up to 7 days in advance or when making reservations

(Keystone Ranch Golf Course cont'd)

Green fees: Seasonal $75 to $95 guests, seasonal $80 to $110 non-guest, including cart

Facility includes: Clubhouse, pro shop, driving range, chipping area, putting green, restaurant

Golf packages available.

Legacy Ridge Golf Resort
10801 Legacy Ridge Parkway, Westminster, CO 80030
303-438-8997
Public

Breathtaking views of the Rocky Mountains will enhance your day on Legacy, which is only 20 minutes northwest from downtown Denver. You need accuracy on this fairly new course because this is target golf with plenty of sand and water en route to bent-grass greens. Nature is abundant because the challenging course sits on 19 acres of wetlands and is home to wildlife, wildflowers, and native grasses.

Yardage: 5,383 to 7,251 / 4 sets of tees

Par: 72

Open: Year-round

Tee times: Up to 2 days in advance, longer with reservation card ($48)

Green fees: $25.50 to $29.50 (cart $15 extra per person, $22 for two people)

Facility includes: Clubhouse, pro shop, driving range, putting green, restaurant

Lone Tree Golf Club and Hotel
9808 Sunningdale Boulevard, Littleton, CO 80124
303-799-9940
Public

A former country club course turned public, Lone Tree offers an open but tricky Palmer design, only 15 miles from the city.

The long, links-style layout is tough with water on more than half of the holes and multi-tiered greens that are well guarded by bunkers.

Yardage: 5,340 to 7,012 / 4 sets of tees

Par: 72

Open: Year-round

Tee times: Up to 3 days in advance

Green fees: $55, including cart

Facility includes: Clubhouse, pro shop, driving range, chipping area, putting green, restaurant

Hotel packages available.

Meadow Hills Golf Course
3609 South Dawson Street, Aurora, CO 80014
303-690-2500
303-397-1818 tee times
Public

Meadow Hills is a country club turned public course with tennis courts and swimming pool still available. It is a walkable, traditional layout with well-placed bunkers, some water, multi-tiered greens, tree-lined fairways, and a nice variety of holes. A stone's throw from Denver, the 40-year-old course is both long and scenic. Accuracy counts.

Yardage: 5,405 to 6,492 / 3 sets of tees

Par: 71/70

Open: Year-round

Tee times: Up to 4 days in advance

Green fees: $22 Monday through Thursday, $24 Friday through Sunday (cart $11 for one person, $20 for two people)

Facility includes: Clubhouse, pro shop, driving range, putting green, restaurant

Works with local hotels.

Plum Creek Golf and Country Club
331 Players Club Drive, Castle Rock, CO 80104
800-488-2612
Semi-Private

Only 45 minutes south of Denver, you'll find this highly rated, well-manicured, links-style course. Not many trees, but enough water and hazards force you to hit straight on this tricky but fair Pete Dye layout complete with medium to large bent-grass greens. Your day can vary dramatically depending on which tees you choose. This course may not be friendly to new players.

Yardage: 4,881 to 7,118 / 4 sets of tees

Par: 72

Open: Year-round

Tee times: Up to 5 days in advance

Green fees: $65 Monday through Thursday, $85 Friday through Sunday, including cart

Facility includes: Clubhouse, pro shop, indoor and outdoor driving range, chipping area, putting green, restaurant

Riverdale Golf Club
13300 Riverdale Road, Brighton, CO 80601
303-659-6700
Public

Two 18-hole courses, including the Dunes and Knoll, are featured at Riverdale. The Dunes, a Scottish links-style course, meanders along a river and insists you hit the ball straight or lose it. Pot bunkers, mounds, and water abound. The Knoll course is a traditional park-style design with plenty of sand, trees, and elevated greens. The Knoll is better suited for new players or high handicappers. Riverdale is 10 miles north of Denver.

Yardage: Dunes, 4,903 to 7,030; Knoll, 5,931 to 6,756 / 4 sets of tees on Dunes; 3 sets of tees on Knoll

Par: Dunes, 72; Knoll, 73/71

Open: Year-round

Tee times: Up to 2 days in advance for weekdays after 7 a.m., for Saturdays, prior Monday after 5:30 p.m., for Sunday, prior Tuesday after 5:30 p.m.

Green fees: Dunes, $27.50 (cart $22 extra), Knoll, $18 (cart $17 extra)

Facility includes: Clubhouse, pro shop, driving range, putting green

---

Wellshire Golf Course
3333 South Colorado Boulevard, Denver, CO 80222
303-757-1352
Public

Built in 1927, Wellshire is another former country club course complete with plenty of trees on a short, tight, tough layout. This one is harder than it looks with subtle rolling hills and a lot of well-situated bunkers. It is also popular because it is located right smack-dab in the city.

Yardage: 5,890 to 6,600 / 3 sets of tees

Par: 73/71

Open: Year-round

Tee times: Up to 3 days in advance, up to 5 days in advance for city residents

Green fees: $20 (cart $22 extra)

Facility includes: Clubhouse, pro shop, driving range, chipping area, putting green, restaurant

Willis Case Golf Course

4999 Vrain Street, Denver, CO 80212
303-455-9801
303-784-4000 tee times (for all city courses)
Public

A pleasant 70-year-old course, Willis Case is a hilly, open lay-out with some pine trees and fairly large greens of moderate speed. Easily accessible and walkable, the course borders on the streets of Denver and is popular for mid-day golf breaks from the office.

Yardage: 6,306 to 6,122 / 2 sets of tees

Par: 75/72

Open: Year-round

Tee times: Up to 3 days in advance, up to 5 days in advance for city residents

Green fees: $20 (carts $20 extra)

Facility includes: Clubhouse, pro shop, chipping area, putting green, restaurant and grill

Hilton Head

Houston

Hilton Head

Hilton Head island on the southern end of South Carolina sports more than 20 courses on and around the island. Originally founded more than 320 years ago, the 4-by-12-mile island is now a prime location for vacationers and meeting planners with hotels and resorts, including Hyatt, Hilton, Westin, Radisson, Best Western, Comfort Inn, and others offering accommodations and golf packages. Property management companies also rent villas, condos, and homes while including golf in your plans.

Peak season is the spring, and resorts can help you make arrangements with most of the area courses. Many reciprocal deals allow you to stay at one hotel and play at most of the others. It's hard to select the best layouts in a golfing rich area such as Hilton Head, so here are a few of the many prime courses.

Harbour Town Golf Links

11 Lighthouse Lane, Hilton Head Island, SC 29925

800-955-8337 tee times

843-363-4485

Resort/Public

A scenic and challenging course, Harbour Town has tight fairways, deep bunkers, thick rough, trees, and small, often well-bunkered greens. The grass is either Bermuda or bent grass, depending on the time of the year. This very highly rated, demanding layout tests all aspects of your game.

Yardage: 5,019 to 6,913 / 3 sets of tees

Par: 71

Open: Year-round

Tee times: Up to 30 days in advance

Green fees: $129 for Seapines guests, $179 for non-guests

Facility includes: Clubhouse, pro shop, driving range, chipping area, putting green, warm-up range, restaurant

Packages with resort and other area resort rental companies.

Hilton Head National Golf Club

P.O. Box 23227, Hilton Head, SC 29925

888-955-1234 tee times

843-842-5900

Public

Hilton Head National, on the site of the historic Lexington Plantation, provides long, tight, rolling, yet forgiving fairways. Cut out of the forest, the 300-acre layout features carefully placed hazards on a well-designed Gary Player course, which includes a unique, huge double green linking the 9th and 18th holes.

Yardage: 4,649 to 6,779 / 4 sets of tees

Par: 72

Open: Year-round

Tee times: Up to 1 year in advance

Green fees: Seasonal from $49 to $100, including cart

Facility includes: Charming old clubhouse, pro shop, driving range, putting green, grill

---

Palmetto Dunes Resort
P.O. Box 5849, Hilton Head Island, SC 29928
800-827-3006 tee times
843-785-1140
Resort

Three courses named for three top golf-course architects are featured at Palmetto. The Arthur Hills course is a tight course that requires precise shot-making skills, whereas the Jones course is a links-style layout that plays toward the ocean and then hooks back in. The Fazio layout is tough and longer and features a lot of sand. All three play around, over, and through a lagoon.

Yardage: Hills, 5,000 to 6,651; Jones, 5,425 to 6,710; Fazio, 5,273 to 6,875 / 3 sets of tees on Jones and Hills; 4 sets of tees for Fazio

Par: Jones and Hills, 72; Fazio, 70

Open: Year-round

Tee times: Up to 60 days in advance

Green fees: Hills and Jones, $75 to $110; Fazio, $60 to $90, including cart

Facility includes: Clubhouse, pro shop, driving ranges, restaurant, 3 miles of ocean

Packages with on-property Hyatt or Hilton or with Palmetto Dunes villas and condos.

Palmetto Hall Plantation

108 Fort Howell Drive, Hilton Head Island, SC 29926

800-827-3006 tee times

843-689-4100

Public

Two designer courses sit on this plantation, including one by Robert Cupp and another named for, and built by, Arthur Hills. The Hills course is a scenic woods course built on an animal preserve. Without many parallel holes, the long layout is spread out and makes use of all natural hazards. The Robert Cupp course is slightly longer with wider, generous fairways. A tribute to the computer world, the geometrically designed course has sharp angles and pyramid-shaped fairways. The rather new course plays very well with almost all holes including marsh or water.

Yardage: Hills, 4,956 to 6,918; Cupp, 5,200 to 7,079 / 4 sets of tees each

Par: 72

Open: Year-round

Tee times: Up to 90 days in advance

Green fees: Seasonal from $85 to $70, including cart

Facility includes: Clubhouse, pro shop, driving range, 2 putting greens, restaurant, snack bars

Discounts for Palmetto Dunes guests and deals with many area resorts.

Houston

A mix of both flat and tree-lined courses, including Scottish-style links layouts and those with some serious elevation changes, Houston offers some great courses. Unfortunately, there aren't enough courses to meet the demand because the city has one of the lowest course-per-golfer ratios of all major markets.

On the bright side, and sometimes it's too bright, golf is playable almost year-round with the possible exception of July and August when it can get too hot.

Hotels can help make tee times, but because many of the courses are outside the immediate area, you might prefer going on your own. *Gulf Coast Golf Magazine* by Golfer Magazines Inc. provides information on golf in the area, and its course map will direct you to the courses. You can find the magazine at courses and the maps in hotels and other visitor locations.

Bay Forest Golf Course
203 Bay Forest Drive, Laporte, TX 77571
281-471-4653
Public

About 30 minutes southeast of Houston sits Bay Forest. The scenic course offers a heavy dose of water on 16 holes plus plenty of woods, particularly on the front nine. This is a short course that is loaded with challenges at very reasonable rates.

Yardage: 5,094 to 6,757 / 3 sets of tees

Par: 72/71

Open: Year-round

Tee times: Call Monday for next 7 days

Green fees: $12 weekdays, $18 weekends (carts $18 extra)

Facility includes: Clubhouse, pro shop, driving range, chipping area, putting green, restaurant

Members can pay $900 per year for unlimited green fees.

The Falls Country Club
1001 North Falls Drive, New Ulm, TX 78950
409-992-3128
Resort/Semi-Private

About 60 miles west of Houston, this top-rated, challenging course offers a wide variety of holes assured to keep the golfer interested. Eleven holes have water, and all include sand. Part of the course is hilly, and most of it is tree-lined.

(The Falls Country Club cont'd)

Yardage: 6,188 to 6,765 / 5 sets of tees

Par: 73/72

Open: Year-round (closed Tuesdays)

Tee times: Up to 4 days in advance

Green fees: $52 Monday through Thursday, $72 Friday through Sunday, including cart

Facility includes: Clubhouse, pro shop, driving range, putting green, snack bar, restaurant

Ask about packages with resort.

Greatwood Golf Club
6767 Greatwood Parkway, Sugar Land, TX 77477
201-343-9999
888-343-4001 tee times
Public

Only 20 miles southeast of the city, this course is rated in the top five public courses in the Houston area. The tight, tree-lined fairways offer target golf with plenty of sand, plus water coming into play on 14 holes.

Yardage: 5,290 to 6,829 / 4 sets of tees

Par: 71

Open: Year-round

Tee times: Up to 3 days in advance

Green fees: $44 weekdays, $58 weekends, including cart

Facility includes: Clubhouse, pro shop, driving range, putting green, bar and grill

Houston Oaks Golf Club
Hegar Road, Huckley, TX 77447
409-931-2917
800-865-4657
Public

Houston Oaks offers two different courses just over 30 minutes from downtown Houston in a country setting. The Oaks is a tree-lined, wooded golf course with some water, whereas the Links is an open links-style layout with wide fairways and high roughs. The second half of the Links course cheats a little with some wooded holes.

Yardage: Oaks, 5,396 to 6,420; Links, 5,011-6397 / 3 sets of tees each

Par: Oaks, 72/71; Links, 72

Open: Year-round

Tee times: One day in advance weekdays, prior Thursday 9:00 a.m. weekends

Green fees: Oaks, $37 Monday through Thursday, $41 Friday, $52 weekends; Links, $32 Monday through Thursday, $39 Friday, $48 weekends

Facility includes: Clubhouse, pro shop, driving range, putting green, restaurant, snack bar

Southwyck Golf Club
2901 Clubhouse Drive, Perland, TX 77584
713-436-9999
Public

One of the best links-style courses in Texas, Southwyck is only 10 miles from Houston. The course features typical wind on a sprawling Scottish-style links design with hazards, tough roughs, and a lot of water. Southwyck is consistently rated one of the top 10 public facilities in the Houston area.

Yardage: 5,211 to 7,000 / 4 sets of tees

Par: 72

Open: Year-round

Tee times: Up to 7 days in advance, up to 2 weeks in advance if a member

Green fees: $44 weekdays, $57 weekends, including cart

Facility includes: Clubhouse, pro shop, full-service driving range, chipping area, putting green, grill, banquet facilities

Area hotels can arrange tee times.

Waterwood National Resort and Country Club
One Waterwood, Huntsville, TX 77340
409-891-5050
800-441-5211
Resort/Public

This course borders Lake Livingstone, and it is a beauty. The scenic, challenging course is ranked as one of the five best in Texas. A wide variety of shots are required with eight holes having water. The tree-lined fairways range from generous to stingy, depending on the hole and the tee. A lot of elevation changes keep it interesting. Waterwood is an hour and a half outside of Houston.

Yardage: 5,029 to 6,872 / 4 sets of tees

Par: 73/71

Open: Year-round

Tee times: Up to 7 days in advance or when making resort reservations

Green fees: $40 weekdays, $60 weekends, including cart

Facility includes: Clubhouse, pro shop, driving range, chipping areas, putting green, golf school, restaurant, conference facilities

Wedgewood Golf Club
5454 Highway 105, West Conroe, TX 77304
409-441-4653
Public

Looking for a tough course in the Houston area? The 50-mile drive brings you to what may be the toughest. Very tight fairways, doglegs everywhere, and undulations on both fairways and greens typify the layout. Throw in some sand traps and water, and you have this challenging golf course.

Yardage: 5,071 to 6,817 / 4 sets of tees

Par: 72

Open: Year-round

Tee times: Up to 7 days in advance for weekdays, prior Wednesdays for weekends

Green fees: $36 Monday through Thursday, $42 Friday, $50 weekends, including cart

Facility includes: Clubhouse, pro shop, driving range, putting green

---

The Woodlands Resort and Country Club
2301 North Millbend Drive, The Woodlands, TX 77380
713-367-1100
Resort/Public

The Woodlands offers two challenging courses open for public play, the North course and the TPC course. The North course is challenging with tree-lined fairways and some very long holes featuring plenty of sand and large bunkers. The TPC course is the site of the Shell Houston Open and is a tournament-style golf course with a lot of water; make sure your drives are accurate.

Yardage: North, 6,339 to 6,880; TPC, 5,302 to 7,045 / 4 sets of tees on North; 3 sets of tees on TPC

Par: 72

Open: Year-round

Tee times: Up to 7 days in advance for weekdays, Wednesday for Saturday, Thursday for Sunday, with resort reservations

Green fees: North, $62 weekdays, $72 weekends, including cart; TPC, seasonal from $75 to $120, including cart

Facility includes: Clubhouse, pro shop, driving range, chipping area, putting green, golf training center, restaurants and convention facilities

Resort packages and memberships to area executives.

Las Vegas

Los Angeles and Vicinity

Las Vegas

One of the most exciting places for business or pleasure, Las Vegas ranks golf second only to the casino action as the favorite pastime. Summer rates are low while temperatures are high, which can be prohibitive. The resort courses offer packages for hotel guests, and other area courses, which are less pricey, provide challenging play and are sometimes less crowded. Hotels are usually helpful at steering you to the courses. Twilight might be a good time to play after business and before evening shows. On Demand sedan service provides clubs for up to five players and access to all area courses.

Vegas courses vary in style; not all are the desert sand and target golf variety. They are very scenic, often long, and in pristine condition. Many are championship-level courses designed by the top course architects in the world. These high-end courses offer top service, including forecaddies and other amenities. They do get a great deal of play, so book ahead. Plan to bring along liquid for the heat and guard against the sun.

Angel Park Golf Club
100 South Rampart Boulevard, Las Vegas, NV 89109
702-254-4653
Public

Only 20 minutes from the casino action, Angel Park offers two solid 18-hole courses. The Arnold Palmer–designed Mountain course is a scenic gem that plays overlooking Red Rock Mountain. The course offers subtle elevation changes with narrow fairways, four water holes, and an excellent finishing hole. You can also find outstanding practice facilities at Angel Park. The Palm course overlooks the city and demands that you stay on the tight fairways. Numerous pine and palm trees keep you on line heading toward fast greens.

Yardage: Mountain, 5,164 to 6,722; Palm, 4,570 to 6,530 / 4 sets of tees each

Par: Mountain 72/71; Palm 70

Open: Year-round

Tee times: Up to 30 days in advance

Green fees: Seasonal from $55 to 110, including cart

Facility includes: Clubhouse, pro shop, driving range, 18-hole putting course, practice areas, including sand traps, 12-hole par 3 lighted course, restaurant, patio dining

Forthcoming neighboring hotel will offer packages; area hotels can arrange tee times.

Desert Inn Golf Club
3145 Las Vegas Boulevard South, Las Vegas, NV 89109
800-634-6909
Resort/Public

The PGA, the Seniors, and the LPGA have played here, and so should you if you're in the area. A classic-style old course, the Desert Inn is long with four 500-yarders from the back tees. The layout offers a little of everything—generous and tight fairways, forgiving and treacherous greens, well-placed bunkers, water, and enough trees to force players to use all their clubs—plus a lot of strategy. The service is first rate.

Yardage: 5,884 to 7,193 / 4 sets of tees

Par: 72

Open: Year-round

Tee times: Up to 90 days in advance for weekdays, up to 7 days in advance for weekends, up to 1 year in advance for hotel guests

Green fees: $215, including cart, for non-guests; $150, including cart, for hotel guests

Facility includes: Clubhouse, pro shop, driving range, putting green, restaurant

*Hotel packages with Desert Inn; discount rate
with Caesar's ($185).*

Desert Rose Golf Club
5483 Clubhouse Drive, Las Vegas, NV 89014
702-431-4653
Public

A $2 million facelift has made this an inviting, attractive course once again. A fairly basic layout, the course offers a traditional setting with a hint of desert golf. Trees, traps, water, and all the basics preside on a fairly short layout, which is less expensive and sometimes easier to get on than its higher-end neighbors.

Yardage: 5,458 to 6,511 / 3 sets of tees

Par: 71

Open: Year-round

Tee times: Up to 7 days in advance for weekdays, up to 3 days in advance for weekends

Green fees: Seasonal from $38 to $75, including cart; rates also depend on the time of day

Facility includes: Clubhouse, pro shop, driving range, snack bar, putting, chipping, sand

Las Vegas Paiute Resort

10325 Nu-Wav Kaiv Boulevard, Las Vegas, NV 89124

800-711-2833

Public

Two Pete Dye long courses, Snow Mountain and Sun Mountain, are both links- and desert-style courses with turf from tee to green on most holes. Although there are few forced carries, there are several water holes and a variety of tricky bunkers as you approach bent-grass greens. Beautiful scenery surrounds these courses.

Yardage: Snow Mountain, 5,341 to 7,158; Sun Mountain, 5,450 to 7,112 / 4 sets of tees each

Par: 72

Open: Year-round

Tee times: Up to 60 days in advance

Green fees: $62 to $125, including cart

Facility includes: Large clubhouse, pro shop, driving range, putting green, restaurant, snack bar

Packages with several local resorts.

The Legacy Golf Club

130 Par Excellence Drive, Henderson, NV

702-897-2187

Public

A links-style Arthur Hills course, the Legacy includes a lake on each nine and lava rock out of bounds. The highly rated course, geared for the power hitters, is one of the longest in a state abundant with courses. The Legacy is only 15 minutes or one long tee shot from the action.

Yardage: 5,340 to 7,233 / 4 sets of tees

Par: 72

Open: Year-round

Tee times: Up to 7 days in advance, up to one year in advance for groups of 20 or more

Green fees: Seasonal from $75 to $125, including cart

Facility includes: Clubhouse, pro shop, driving range, putting green, restaurant, banquet facilities

Golf packages include luxury transportation to and from resorts.

Las Vegas National Golf Club
1911 East Desert Inn Road, Las Vegas, NV 89109
702-734-1796
800-468-7918 tee times
Resort/Public

A major tournament stop for the pros, this old gem has stood the test of time. Five lakes, plenty of palms (and other trees) on an open layout, and well-bunkered greens provide a challenge for players at all levels. Computerized golf carts are fun and helpful as they gage yardage.

Yardage: 5,741 to 6,815 / 4 sets of tees

Par: 71

Open: Year-round

Tee times: Up to 60 days in advance

Green fees: Seasonal from $75 to $175, including cart

Facility includes: Clubhouse, pro shop, driving range, practice area, restaurant

Packages for three days of play, including four other area courses.

Oasis Resort Hotel Casino
851 Oasis Boulevard, Mesquite, Nevada 89024
800-621-0187
Resort

If you venture just over an hour northwest of the Vegas Strip, you'll find the Oasis Golf Course, complete with dramatic elevation changes, canyon holes, great scenery, and plenty of sand. Adjacent, you'll find the lengthy Palms course composed of two unique nines, water holes, major hills, and some tough par 5s that will let you wind up and air it all out.

Yardage: Oasis, 4,659 to 6,982; Palms, 5,016 to 7,008 / 4 sets of tees each

Par: 72

Open: Year-round

Tee times: Up to 60 days in advance

Green fees: Seasonal from $50 to $100 for hotel guests, $60 to $125 non-guests, including cart

Facility includes: Clubhouse, pro shop, driving range, practice facility, 9-hole par 3 course, deli

Several group packages, including two-night plans with golf, also membership plans.

Painted Desert Golf Club
5555 Painted Mirage Drive, Las Vegas, NV 89129
702-645-2568
Public

Set in a beautiful, natural desert landscape, this meticulously maintained course has target fairways and challenging greens. Beautiful mountain scenery flanks this layout, which is only 20 minutes from the Strip.

Yardage: 5,711 to 6,840 / 3 sets of tees

Par: 72

Open: Year-round

Tee times: Up to 60 days in advance through hotels

Green fees: $70 to $130 depending on season, time of day, residence, and so on. All include cart.

Facility includes: Clubhouse, pro shop, driving range, chipping area, putting green, restaurant

Packages with Santa Fe Hotel

Rhodes Ranch Golf Club

9020 Rhodes Ranch Parkway, Las Vegas, NV 89113

702-740-4114

www.rhodesranch.com

Public

A long new course, it's both scenic and challenging with elevated fast greens and water on nearly half the holes. Fair to all level of players, shorter hitters can spray the ball, but longer hitters are forced to keep it straight as the fairways narrow. Long par 3s, mostly over water, will test you on this tough but fun course.

Yardage: 5,800 to 6,990 / 5 sets of tees

Par: 72

Open: Year-round

Tee times: Up to 60 days in advance

Green fees: $99 Monday through Thursday, $125 Friday through Sunday, including cart

Facility includes: Clubhouse, pro shop, driving range, putting green, restaurant, snack bar

Sun City Las Vegas Golf Club
9201-B Del Webb Boulevard, Las Vegas, NV 89128
Palm Valley course, 702-363-4373
Highland Falls course, 702-254-7010
Eagle Crest course, 702-240-1312
Semi-Private

Two diverse long courses and a short executive course make up the Sun City Golf experience. Palm Valley is a traditional course, flat, with some water, and undulating bent-grass greens. Highland Falls offers spectacular views and dramatic elevation changes with wide fairways and tough rough. Eagle Crest is a par 60 executive course for those on a tighter schedule.

Yardage: Highland, 5,100 to 6,512; Palm Valley, 5,502 to 6,849 / 4 sets of tees each

Par: 72

Open: Year-round

Tee times: Up to 7 days in advance

Green fees: $60 to $96, including cart

Facility includes: Clubhouse, pro shop, driving range, chipping area, putting green, restaurants

Tournament Players Club at the Canyons
9851 Canyon Run Drive, Las Vegas, NV 89134
702-256-2500
Resort

The Canyons course is as challenging as it is beautiful. A flawless desert course, TPC sees steady tournament action and is built through natural desert canyons. These canyons provide elevation changes and spectacular views of Red Rock Canyon and the Vegas Strip. Forced carries over the desert and an arroyo (creek) running along the 13th can make this course especially tough from the back tees and for high handicappers.

Yardage: 5,039 to 7,063 / 4 sets of tees

Par: 71

Open: Year-round

Tee times: Up to 30 days in advance, up to 180 days in advance with early booking fee added

Green fees: Seasonal from $74 to $170, including cart

Facility includes: Clubhouse, driving range, putting green, restaurant, snack bars

Forthcoming resort affiliation may provide packages.

Los Angeles and Vicinity

In Los Angeles, everything is spread out, including top courses, which you can find from Malibu to Palm Springs. Although the shore courses include several links layouts, there are also plenty of park- and traditional-style designs. Many area facilities offer more than one course, providing options close to wherever you are staying in or around Los Angeles. In the heart of Los Angeles are a few city courses led by Griffith Park, which are often very crowded. Like its big city neighbor to the south, San Diego, Los Angeles is one of the few areas where you can enjoy golfing year-round. Unlike in most markets, in Los Angeles, you can run into celebrities as you play.

Several local magazines and newspapers feature sections on the courses, and many area hotels can assist you when looking for tee times. The Web site www.scplga.org can also help you when seeking courses, but their prices, in some cases, are dated.

Anaheim Hills Golf Course
6501 Nohl Ranch Road, Anaheim CA 92807
714-748-8900
Public

With more ups and downs than the rides at nearby Disneyland, Anaheim Hills is appropriately named. The tight, lush course has plenty of blind shots and elevated tees and

(Anaheim Hills Golf Course cont'd)

makes good use of the hilly terrain. One of only two city courses in Anaheim, the scenic setting is just 45 minutes from Los Angeles.

Yardage: 5,361 to 6,500 / 3 sets of tees

Par: 72/71

Open: Year-round

Tee times: Up to 7 days in advance

Green fees: $33 weekdays, $39 weekends, including cart

Facility includes: Clubhouse, pro shop, driving range, 2 putting greens, restaurant, snack bar

---

Brookside Golf Course
1133 North Rosemont Avenue, Pasadena, CA 91103
626-796-0177
Public

Adjacent to the Rose Bowl, Brookside offers two old courses. The C.W. Koiner course is long and flat with generous fairways, whereas the E.O. Nay course is shorter with small, tough greens. A few water hazards and well-placed bunkers round out the courses that sit 20 minutes from downtown Los Angeles.

Yardage: Koiner, 6,104 to 7,030; Nay, 5,300 to 6,046 / 4 sets of tees on Koiner; 3 sets of tees on Nay

Par: Koiner, 75/72, Nay, 71/70

Open: Year-round

Tee times: Up to 5 days in advance for weekdays, Mondays for Saturdays, and Tuesdays for Sundays

Green fees: $30 weekdays, $40 weekends (carts $24 extra)

Facility includes: Clubhouse, pro shop, driving range, 2 putting greens, restaurant

Cypress Golf Course
4921 Ketella Avenue, Los Alamitos, CA 90720
714-527-1800
Public

About 30 minutes from Los Angeles, Cypress is a very narrow
course with its fair share of hills and plenty of water found on
most of the 18 holes. Bermuda fairways and bent-grass greens
highlight this challenging, unique layout that insists you hit
it straight.

Yardage: 4,700 to 6,510 / 5 sets of tees

Par: 71

Open: Year-round

Tee time: Up to 7 days in advance

Green fees: $70 weekdays, $90 weekends, including cart

Facility includes: Clubhouse, pro shop, driving range,
putting green, restaurant

DeBell Golf Club
1500 Walnut Avenue, Burbank, CA 91504
818-845-0022
Public

Smack-dab in the heart of beautiful downtown Burbank is
a fun, little layout that is tougher than executive courses
because of the terrain and wide array of hazards. Uphill
fairways, plenty of out of bounds, and tight fairways playing
through the canyons make DeBell play longer than it looks.
Be forewarned; it's not easy to get on for non-Burbank
residents.

Yardage: 5,300 to 5,900 / 2 sets of tees

Par: 73/71

Open: Year-round

Tee times: Up to 3 days in advance unless with Burbank
reservation card

(DeBell Golf Club cont'd)

Green fees: $18 weekdays, $23 weekends (carts $20 extra)

Facility includes: Clubhouse, pro shop, driving range, putting green, restaurant, snack bar

---

Desert Princess Country Club and Resort
28-555 Landau Boulevard, Cathedral City, CA 92234
619-322-2280
Resort

With the Doubletree resort as a backdrop, three well-planned 9-holers make up this sprawling layout on the boarder of Palm Springs. The Vista course is Spanish links-style with mounds and bunkers, whereas Lagos and Cielo are more traditional, tighter courses. All three rather flat courses incorporate water and lead to bent-grass greens.

Yardage: Up to 6,684 depending on configuration / 3 sets of tees

Par: 72

Open: Year-round

Tee times: Up to 2 days in advance, further advance for guests

Green fees: Seasonal from $45 to $120, including cart

Facility includes: Clubhouse, pro shop, driving range, putting green, restaurant, snack bar

Packages with resort.

El Dorado Park Golf Club
2400 Studebaker, Long Beach, CA 90815
562-430-5411
Public

Thirty minutes from Los Angeles, this popular Long Beach course has tree-lined, tight fairways and plenty of elevation changes. The course is tough with tricky little greens. A park setting provides a relaxing, scenic getaway when not drawing a crowd as host for the annual Long Beach Open.

Yardage: 6,518 to 6,481/ 3 sets of tees

Par: 72

Open: Year-round

Tee time: Up to 3 days in advance

Green fees: $18.50 weekdays, $22.50 weekends (carts $10.50 extra per person)

Facility includes: Clubhouse, pro shop, driving range, chipping area, putting green, restaurant

Discounts for Long Beach residents with card.

Griffith Park Golf
4730 Crystal Springs Drive, Los Angeles, CA 90027
213-664-2255
Public

Arguably the best of the Los Angeles city courses, the two 18-hole layouts offer old-fashioned golf. The Wilson course has wide-open fairways, some small hills, and small, slow greens. The Harding course features tall trees and small greens. Both 70-year-old courses are very popular—so prepare to wait.

Yardage: Harding, 6,028 to 6,610; Wilson, 6,483 to 6,945 / 3 sets of tees

Par: Harding, 71; Wilson, 72

Open: Year-round

Tee times: In advance with Los Angeles reservation card only; otherwise, just show up

Green fees: $17.50 weekdays, $23 weekends (carts $20 extra)

Facility includes: Clubhouse, pro shop, driving range, putting green, restaurant and banquet facilities, snack bar

Indian Wells Golf Resort
44500 Indian Wells Lane, Indian Wells, CA 92210
760-346-4653
Public

Two hours from Los Angeles (and two hours from San Diego for that matter), Indian Wells Resort offers two beautiful courses for the large conference and convention crowd that visits the area. Both courses are tight and well maintained with Bermuda fairways and plenty of trees. The West course has some hills but plays shorter than its neighbor to the east, which is also relatively tight. The East course also sports a unique island fairway.

Yardage: West, 5,408 to 6,500; East, 5,516 to 6,631, / 3 sets of tees each

Par: 72

Open: Year-round

Tee times: Up to 7 days in advance, up to 60 days in advance with one of five area hotels

Green fees: $130 weekdays, $140 weekends, including cart

Facility includes: Clubhouse, 2 driving ranges, short-game center, 3 putting greens, restaurant, golf school

Work with Esmerelda, Hyatt, Sands, Hotel Indian Wells, or Mira Monte.

Industry Hills Sheraton Resort and Conference Center
One Industry Hills Parkway, City of Industry, CA 91744
626-854-GOLF
Public

An hour from Los Angeles, these two resort courses provide difficult rounds on well-maintained layouts. The Eisenhower course is hilly and long with major elevation changes and large greens. It's not for the new player or high handicapper. The Zaharis course is much tighter but shorter with fast bent-grass greens. Not as tough as the Eisenhower, the Babe course, as it's called, still insists you hit it straight. Both courses are built on a landfill.

Yardage: Eisenhower, 5,589 to 7,181; Zaharis, 5,262 to 6,778 / 4 sets of tees each

Par: Eisenhower, 72; Zaharis, 71

Open: Year-round

Tee times: Up to 3 days in advance, longer for resort guests

Green fees: $50 Monday through Thursday, $65 Friday through Sunday, including cart

Facility includes: Clubhouse, pro shop, driving range, 4 putting greens, 9-hole par 3 course, restaurant, snack bar

Packages with resort.

La Quinta Resort and Club
50-200 Vista Bonita, La Quinta, CA 92253
760-564-7686
Resort

La Quinta sports a beautiful, typically tough Pete Dye Mountain course with dramatic elevation changes along with a well-bunkered sandy links-style layout. The Mountain course features plenty of red rock and deep rough surrounding manicured greens. The Dunes is flatter with rolling mounds, tough doglegs, and an island green flanked by sand. Both challenging 18-hole courses flank a scenic resort setting only 20 miles from Palm Springs and just over two hours from Los Angeles.

Yardage: Mountain, 5,010 to 6,758; Dunes, 5,005 to 6,747 / 5 sets of tees each

Par: 72

Open: Year-round

Tee times: Inquire when making reservations

(La Quinta Resort and Club cont'd)

Green fees: Mountain, seasonal from $90 to $235; Dunes, $60 to $175, including cart

Facility includes: Clubhouse, pro shop, driving range, chipping area, bunker practice, putting green, restaurant, snack bar

Packages available with resort.

Malibu Country Club
901 Encinial Canyon Road, Malibu, CA 90265
818-889-6680
Public

North of Los Angeles sits this tough layout that plays along the mountainside in the high country and then goes into canyons, providing major elevation changes. Several lakes also come into play on this popular, very well-maintained public facility, which tests all levels of golfers.

Yardage: 5,523 to 6,631 / 3 sets of tees
Par: 72
Open: Year-round
Tee times: Up to 10 days in advance
Green fees: $52 weekdays, $77 weekends, including cart
Facility includes: Clubhouse, pro shop, driving range, putting green, restaurant

Familiar to most area hotels for tee times.

Ojai Valley Inn
Country Club Road, Ojai, CA 93023
805-646-2420
Resort/Public

Just over an hour south of downtown Los Angeles sits Ojai, sporting a first rate course and resort. This picturesque, out-of-the-way layout is not very long but challenging, nonetheless. Plenty of trees, well-placed bunkers, and fast greens typify the setting, which is a rare Southern California course without water. The short par 4s are skillfully designed to test your iron game.

Yardage: 5,225 to 6,235 / 3 sets of tees
Par: 71/70
Open: Year-round
Tee times: Up to 7 days in advance, up to 90 days in advance for resort guests
Green fees: $120, including cart
Facility includes: Clubhouse, pro shop, driving range, putting green, restaurant, snack bar

Packages with resort.

Pelican Hill Golf Course
22651 Pelican Hills Road, Newport Coast, CA 92657
949-759-5190
Resort/Public

About an hour north of Los Angeles sits this ocean-side resort with spectacular views and two first-rate courses. The Ocean North course has rolling hills, plenty of bunkers, high elevation, low vegetation, and thick rough. The neighboring Ocean South course has lower elevation and more vegetation, plays through canyons, and makes good use of all existing terrain.

Yardage: Ocean North, 5,800 to 6,724; Ocean South, 5,409 to 6,636 / 5 sets of tees each
Par: Ocean North 71; Ocean South 70
Open: Year-round
Tee times: Up to 7 days in advance, 48-hour cancellation, premium rates available up to 60 days in advance with $20 fee, guests up to 60 days in advance without additional charge
Green fees: $150 weekdays, $210 weekends, including cart
Facility includes: Award-winning pro shop, driving range, putting green, restaurant, lounge, banquet facilities

Talk to Four Seasons resort about packages.

Miami and South Florida

Minneapolis/St. Paul

Myrtle Beach

Miami and South Florida

Florida is home to nearly 1,000 golf courses, and Miami has long been a popular golfing town, although courses are now being built more often in the northern part of the state. Nonetheless, some resort hotels, in particular the Doral, sport first-rate courses for year-round play. After 35 years, Don Shula's course is still a perennial area favorite. *Fore Florida*, 561-288-7499, is a local magazine that you can find at courses and hotels throughout the state to get information on golf around Florida. The prime season for golf runs from April into the fall.

Colony West Country Club
6800 North West 88th Avenue, Tamarac, FL 33321
954-726-8430
Public

Only 45 minutes from Miami and 20 minutes from Ft. Lauderdale, Colony West is a highly ranked public course with tree-lined, often tight fairways and a lot of water. The long and flat course can be tough for high handicappers, and it provides a good test for the more skilled player.

Yardage: 5,422 to 7,271 / 5 sets of tees

Par: 71

Open: Year-round

Tee times: Up to 7 days in advance

Green fees: Seasonal from $35 to $100, including cart

Facility includes: Clubhouse, pro shop, chipping area, putting green, restaurant, snack bar

Don Shula's Golf Club
7601 Miami Lakes Drive, Miami Lakes, FL 33014
305-821-1150
Public

The Dolphin's former coach opened a course 35 years ago, and it's still going strong. A lot of trees and a Northern look characterize this very Southern course with some water and a nice variety of holes. This popular long course is a few minutes from Miami Beach hotels.

Yardage: 5,600 to 7,035 / 4 sets of tees

Par: 72

Open: Year-round

Tee times: Up to 3 days in advance or with hotel reservation

Green fees: Seasonal from $36 to $50, including cart

Facility includes: Clubhouse, pro shop, driving range, putting green, lighted par 3 course, restaurant, snack bar

Packages with Don Shula Hotel.

Doral Golf Resort and Spa
4400 North West 87th Avenue, Miami, FL 33178
305-592-2000
800-713-6725
Resort/Public

On over 650 acres of land in Miami, just 7 miles from the airport, this conference-center hotel specializes in golf. Five courses include the newly refurbished Silver course and the soon to be closed for renovation White course (which will reopen as Great White in the year 2000). The toughest of the courses, the Blue (or Blue Monster) has plenty of trees, 190 bunkers, water, and large Bermuda greens on an extremely challenging layout designed for the better players. The Gold comes close in terms of water. The Red course is shorter, flatter, and better suited for newer players. The Silver course sports water on every hole with undulating greens, one of which is the island variety.

Yardage: Blue, 5,392 to 7,395; Gold, 5,179 to 6,602; Red, 5,096 to 6,145; Silver, 4,738 to 6,557 / 4 sets of tees each

Par: Blue, 72; Gold, 70; Red, 71; Silver, 71

Open: Year-round

Tee times: Up to 7 days in advance, up to 30 days in advance for resort guests

Green fees: Blue, seasonal from $100 to $240; Gold and Silver, $90 to $200; Red, $80 to $180, including cart; White not open at present

Facility includes: Clubhouse, pro shop, driving range, putting green, 9-hole executive course, restaurant, snack bar, banquet facilities, conference center, membership packages

Resort packages.

Emerald Dunes Golf Club

2100 Emerald Dunes Drive, West Palm Beach, FL 33411

561-684-4653

888-650-4653

www.emeralddunes.com

Public

All right, it's not Miami; it's up the Florida turnpike in West Palm Beach, but it's worth the drive. The 1,000th course built in Florida, Emerald Dunes has absolutely everything you could ask for in a golf course, including rolling hills, dunes, plenty of white-sand bunkers, water all over the place, mounds, native grass and plant life, a few trees, waterfalls, and in-cart computerized, satellite-controlled yardage and course information systems. Providing a country club atmosphere, Emerald is ranked as one of the top public courses in the world.

Yardage: 4,676 to 7,006 / 5 sets of tees

Par: 72

Open: Year-round

Tee times: Up to 30 days in advance

Green fees: Seasonal from $70 to $150, including cart

Facility includes: Clubhouse, pro shop, driving range, chipping areas, putting green, restaurant, banquet facilities

Works with 13 area hotels and resorts.

Jacaranda Golf Club

9200 West Broward Boulevard, Plantation, Florida 33324

954-472-5836

888-955-1234 tee times

Semi-Private

Sitting 12 miles from Ft. Lauderdale, Jacaranda has two beautiful, well-designed courses. The East course has plenty of sand and water and is longer than its neighbor to the west.

Both courses have gently rolling terrain framed by lush foliage and waterways.

Yardage: East, 5,668 to 7,195; West, 5,314 to 6,729 / 4 sets of tees each

Par: 72

Open: Year-round

Tee times: Up to 7 days in advance

Green fees: Seasonal from $53 to $99, including cart

Facility includes: Clubhouse, pro shop, driving range, pitching and chipping area, 4 putting greens, restaurant, banquet facility, snack bar

Packages with area hotels.

Miami Shores Country Club
10000 Biscayne Boulevard, Miami Shores, FL 33138
305-795-2366
Semi-Private

Doglegs and small elevated greens typify this not-too-long, 60-year-old, enjoyable (and walkable) course. Like most Florida courses, the layout is flat with bunkers and water coming into play. A stone's throw from Miami Beach, the Shores sees a great number of players of all levels.

Yardage: 5,400 to 6,400 / 3 sets of tees

Par: 72/71

Open: Year-round

Tee times: Up to 3 days in advance

Green fees: Seasonal from 40 to $60, including cart

Facility includes: Clubhouse, pro shop, driving range, restaurant and banquet facility

Works with local Miami hotels.

PGA National Golf Club

1000 Avenue of Champions, Palm Beach, FL 33418
561-627-1800
www.pgaresorts.com
Resort

A golfer's paradise, PGA National lets you play where the pros play. Five top courses designed by golf legends will test all levels of skill on this facility, which is for resort guests (or members) only. The Champion course, which has seen plenty of tournaments, has woods, water on 16 holes and more than 100 sand bunkers and was expertly designed by Fazio and re-designed by Nicklaus; what more can you say? It's also very hard to get on. The General has undulating fairways, numerous grass and sand bunkers, and water on almost every hole. The Haig sports nearly 70 sand bunkers and also has a lot of water. The Squire is a shorter position course where accuracy counts. The Estate course is newer and a little shorter but has its share of hazards. The courses are all well maintained with all details taken care of. PGA National is two hours north of Miami.

Yardage: Championship, 5,377 to 6,742; Squire, 4,975 to 6,465; Haig, 5,645 to 6,806; General, 5,327 to 6,768; Estate, 4,955 to 6,784 / Championship, 4 sets of tees; others, 3 sets of tees each

Par: 72

Open: Year-round

Tee times: Inquire when making room reservation

Green fees: Included in hotel packages, including carts

Facility includes: Clubhouse, pro shop, driving range, chipping area, putting greens, golf school, restaurant, snack bars

Numerous packages.

Minneapolis/St. Paul

Courses in the region are primarily built within and around their natural terrain, which features trees and grasses native to the area, lakes, and wildlife.

The golf season runs from April through October, and the popularity of golf is increasing during those months, so call ahead. Within an hour from the Minneapolis/St. Paul area are resorts and public courses, mostly at reasonable rates. The Minnesota Golf Association, 612-927-4643, can provide you with a more detailed directory and map to area courses. You can also look them up at www.mngolf.org.

Although some of the major downtown area hotels can help with tee times, because many of the courses are out of the immediate area, you may prefer calling on your own. When playing in and around Minneapolis/St. Paul, bring extra balls because numerous lakes and streams can prove hazardous to your game.

To obtain tee times and information for five Minneapolis city courses (and a few others), you can call a main number at 612-949-4949.

Bunker Hills Golf Course
Highway 242 and Foley Boulevard, Coon Rapids, MN 55448
612-755-4141
Public

Just over 30 minutes north of Minneapolis sits the 27-hole Bunker Hills layout. The East and West nines offer wide-open fairways with forgiving landing areas. Plenty of well-placed bunkers and some water will keep you alert en route to tricky greens. The North course is tightly wooded with plenty of pine trees plus some bunkers to boot. All three are popular and challenging courses.

Yardage: 5,622 to 6,535 / 4 sets of tees

Par: 72

Open: April through November

(Bunker Hills Golf Course cont'd)

Tee times: Up to 3 days in advance after 11 a.m.

Green fees: $35, $30 for soft or no spikes (carts $24 extra)

Facility includes: Clubhouse, pro shop, driving range, putting green, additional executive 9-hole course, restaurant

---

Crystal Lakes Golf Course
16725 Innsbrook Drive, Lakeville, MN 55044
612-432-6566
Public

Crystal Lakes features two distinct nines. The front has rolling hills and plenty of elevation changes, whereas the back nine sits on reclaimed wetlands and offers wildlife, and natural terrain indigenous to the region. The four-year-old facility sits just 15 minutes south of The Mall of America to complete your golfing and shopping day.

Yardage: 4,805 to 6,306 / 3 sets of tees

Par: 71

Open: April through October

Tee times: Up to 3 days in advance or prepaid up to 7 days in advance

Green fees: $23 weekdays, $29 weekends (cart $11 extra per person)

Facility includes: Clubhouse, driving range, practice holes, snack bar

---

Edinburgh USA Golf Club
8700 Edienbrook Crossing, Brooklyn Park, MN 55443
612-424-7060
Public

A lot of sand, tough rough, and plenty of water characterize this challenging target golf layout only 12 miles north of downtown Minneapolis. This popular course is highly rated and extremely well maintained.

Yardage: 5,255 to 6,700 / 4 sets of tees

Par: 72

Open: April through October

Tee times: Up to 4 days in advance, after 2 p.m. for groups of 3 or 4

Green fees: $36 (cart $26 extra)

Facility includes: Clubhouse, pro shop, driving range, chipping area, putting green, restaurant

---

Fox Hollow Golf Course
478 Palmgren Lane North East, Rogers, MN 55374
612-428-4468
Semi-Private

Fox Hollow is a riverside links-style course with bent-grass everything, plenty of sand, and an island hole to make things interesting. If you like water, it's worth the 40-minute ride from the city—which is also quite scenic.

Yardage: 5,161 to 6,726 / 4 sets of tees

Par: 72

Open: April through Mid November

Tee times: Up to 3 days in advance

Green fees: $27 weekdays, $33 weekends (cart $11 extra per person)

Facility includes: Clubhouse, pro shop, driving range, putting green, restaurant, banquet facilities

---

Francis A. Gross Golf Course
2201 St. Anthony Boulevard, Minneapolis, MN 55418
612-789-2542
Public

This old course still has a lot of kick to it with mature trees lining most of the fairways and a little water because it is, after all, Minneapolis. It's well advised to be accurate hitting on this easily accessible, busy city course.

(Francis A. Gross Golf Course cont'd)

Yardage: 5,257 to 6,574 / 4 sets of tees

Par: 71

Open: April through November

Tee times: Up to 4 days in advance, 24-hour cancellation policy

Green fees: $21 (cart $22 extra plus $5 refundable key deposit)

Facility includes: Clubhouse, chipping area, putting green, snack bar

---

Grand View Lodge
South 134 Nokomis, Misswa, MN 56468
800-432-3788
218-963-2234
www.thepines.com
Resort

Flanking an 80-year-old lodge are 45 holes of championship golf on 18- and 27-hole courses. The 27-hole, award-winning Pines layout has 3 distinct 9-hole setups. The Lakes and Marsh nines have plenty of water on each, and the Woods nine is cut out of the forest with deer and elk passing through. The new Preserve course is a beautiful layout on 240 acres, featuring three dozen sand traps, 40 acres of wetlands, plenty of trees, and several elevation changes. The resort courses are two hours from the Minneapolis/St. Paul area and are well worth taking a couple of days to visit. This is one of many courses becoming soft-spike-only facilities.

Yardage: Pines, 5,112 to 6,683, depending on configuration; Preserve, 4,816 to 6,601 / 4 sets of tees on Pines; 3 sets of tees on Preserve

Par: 72

Open: April through mid October

Tee times: Up to 2 days in advance, up to 1 year in advance with confirmed lodge reservation, 24-hour cancellation policy

Green fees: Pines, $53.50 Monday through Thursday, $63.50 Friday through Sunday; Preserve, $43.50 Monday through Thursday, $49.50 weekends, including cart

Facility includes: Clubhouse, award-winning pro shop, driving range, practice bunkers, putting green, par 3 9-hole course, restaurant and grill

Resort offers several packages.

Keller Golf Course
2166 Maplewood Drive, St. Paul, MN 55109
651-484-3011
Public

Scenic, gently rolling, tree-lined fairways with a lot of bunkers and a little water define Keller, which is an above-average, 70-year-old fun course.

Yardage: 5,373 to 6,500 / 3 sets of tees

Par: 73/72

Open: April through October

Tee times: Up to 4 days in advance

Green fees: $23 (cart $22 extra)

Facility includes: Clubhouse, pro shop, driving range, putting green, restaurant

The Links at Northfork
9333 153rd Avenue Northwest, Ramsey, MN 55307
612-241-0506
Public

If you don't like trees, this one's for you—almost no trees to be found. Water, mounds, wind, and plenty of trouble typify this Scottish links-style layout, only 20 miles from Minneapolis.

(The Links at Northfork cont'd)

Yardage: 5,242 to 6,989 / 4 sets of tees

Par: 72

Open: April through October

Tee times: Up to 7 days in advance

Green fees: $29 weekdays, $35 weekends (cart $12 extra per person)

Facility includes: Clubhouse, driving range, practice holes, snack bar

Works with Northland Inn.

Stonebrooke Golf Club
2693 County Road 79, Shakopee, MN 55379
612-496-3171
Semi-Private

A lot of old trees, plenty of elevation changes, quite a few doglegs, and a good amount of water make Stonebrooke difficult. The layout, scenery, and country-club–look make the course very appealing and worth the 25-mile trip from downtown Minneapolis, which includes a ferry ride.

Yardage: 5,033 to 6,604 / 4 sets of tees

Par: 72

Open: April through October

Tee times: Up to 3 days in advance

Green fees: $31 weekdays, $38 weekends (cart $26 extra)

Facility includes: Clubhouse, pro shop, driving range, putting green, executive course, restaurant

Popular with area hotels for bookings.

Theodore Wirth Golf Course
1300 Theodore Wirth Parkway, Minneapolis, MN 55422
612-522-4584
Public

The granddaddy of the lakes region, this old course features many mature trees, a lot of water, some hills, and tough little greens. Basic no-frills golf, Theodore is a very accessible solid city layout.

Yardage: 5,313 to 6,548 / 4 sets of tees

Par: 72

Open: April through November

Tee times: Up to 4 days in advance, 24-hour cancellation policy

Green fees: $21 (cart $22 extra)

Facility includes: Clubhouse, putting green, snack bar

The Wilds Golf Club
3151 Wilde Ridge, Prior Lake, MN 55372
612-445-4455
Public

The Wilds is one of the newest courses in the Minneapolis area, about 30 minutes from downtown. A traditional layout, the course is complete with pine trees, wetlands, bunkers, and wildlife because it incorporates a wildlife habitat.

Yardage: 5,095 to 7,028 / 5 sets of tees

Par: 72

Open: April through October

Tee times: Up to 14 days in advance for foursomes or 5 days for others

Green fees: $99, including cart

Facility includes: Clubhouse, pro shop, 2-ended driving range, chipping area, putting green, restaurant

Myrtle Beach

Myrtle Beach courses are situated between Carolina woodlands and lakes with water holes, insisting you bring plenty of extra balls. More than 90 courses are available in the area, which has been billed as the "Seaside Golf Capital of the World" with 4 million rounds played annually. Information and a golf-planning guide are available for the area through the tourist office, and you can look online at www.myrtlebeach-info.com for more details.

Peak season is the spring, and Myrtle Beach resorts are familiar with the numerous courses and help make your golfing experience first rate. Many reciprocal deals allow you to stay at one hotel and play at most of the others. It's hard to narrow down the field in golfing areas such as these, but here are a few of the many marvelous layouts.

Arrowhead Golf Club
1201 Burcale Road, Myrtle Beach, SC 29577
843–236–3243
Public

Nestled in the trees are three 9-hole courses built along the banks of the Intercoastal Waterway that divides the Arrowhead golfing complex. Sloping fairways characterize the Lakes course, the Cypress course plays along the wetlands, and the Waterway course has plenty of, you guessed it, water. All three courses have well-bunkered bent-grass greens. Arrowhead is close to the major resorts and only a few minutes from the Myrtle Beach airport.

Yardage: 4,812 to 6,666 / 4 sets of tees
Par: 72
Open: Year-round
Tee times: Arbitrary during off season, with prepayment during peak season
Green fees: Seasonal from $42 to $78, including cart
Facility includes: Clubhouse, pro shop, driving range, chipping area, putting green, grill

Packages with most area hotels.

Bay Tree Golf Plantation

P.O. Box 240, Highway 9, North Myrtle Beach, SC 29597

800-845-6191

843-249-1487

Public

Three spectacular, sprawling 18-hole courses are spread out across the plantation. The Gold course features rolling hills, white sand, and waterways. The long Green course will let you muscle the ball, but the water, tree-lined fairways, and well-placed bunkers will also test your accuracy. The Silver course, recently upgraded, has a links feel. There are a few tree-lined fairways, but otherwise, it is a fairly open layout.

Yardage: Gold, 5,264 to 6,942; Green, 5,362 to 7,044; Silver, 5,417 to 6,871 / 3 sets of tees each

Par: 72

Open: Year-round

Tee times: Up to 1 year in advance, prepayment for more than 48 hours

Green fees: Seasonal from $35 to $70, including cart

Facility includes: Clubhouse, pro shop, driving range, 2 putting greens, snack bar

Works with about 100 area hotels on packages.

Belle Terre Golf Course

4073 U.S. Highway 501, Myrtle Beach, SC 29577

800-340-0072

843-236-8888

Public

This brand new Rees Jones gem offers great golf in a gorgeous southern setting. The Championship course is a sprawling layout with sparkling lakes and wetlands bordering several holes. A long course, Belle has character with mounds galore and white-sand bunkers around tough greens. Some holes are wide-open holes, but others play through the pine trees of

(Belle Terre Golf Course cont'd)

the region. Well situated, the course is close to both the resorts and the Myrtle Beach airport.

Yardage: 5,049 to 7,013 / 5 sets of tees

Par: 72

Open: Year-round

Tee times: Up to 1 year in advance

Green fees: Seasonal from $58 to $91, including cart

Facility includes: Clubhouse, pro shop, driving range, 2 putting greens, 18-hole executive course, restaurant

Packages with area hotels.

Caledonia Golf and Fish Club
369 Caledonia Drive, Pawleys Island, SC 29585
803-237-3675
Public

A classic new course, Caledonia sits 30 minutes from Myrtle Beach but is beginning to draw a lot of players with its strong reputation. A tight course, featuring oak tree-lined fairways, Caledonia has a lot of sand, plenty of waste bunkers, and a little water on a sprawling plantation setting. No fishing!

Yardage: 4,968 to 6,503 / 4 sets of tees

Par: 70

Open: Year-round

Tee times: Up to 1 year in advance

Green fees: Seasonal from $65 to $120, including cart

Facility includes: Clubhouse, pro shop, driving net, putting green, restaurant, snack bar

Golf packages with resorts.

The Dunes West Golf Club
3535 Wando Plantation Way, Mt. Pleasant, SC 29464
800-591-5809
843-856-9000
Semi-Private

Dunes West is in the center of South Carolina with open fairways, large greens, and 200-year-old oak trees typical of the area. The course sits on a sprawling plantation only 10 miles from Charleston. A well-designed layout with a lot of sand and bunkers, the course is fun and challenging for golfers of varying levels.

Yardage: 5,278 to 6,871 / 3 sets of tees

Par: 72

Open: Year-round

Tee times: Up to 90 days in advance

Green fees: Seasonal from $35 to $80, including cart

Facility includes: Clubhouse, pro shop, driving range, putting green, restaurant

Packages with area hotels.

The Legends Resort
Highway 501, Myrtle Beach, SC 29578-0516
800-990-8995
843-236-9318
Resort/Public

Three distinctive 18-hole courses make up the Legends. The Heathland is modeled after the classic Royal and Ancient Golf Club in Scotland. Mounds, dunes, pot bunkers, and rolling fairways with wind and no trees characterize this tricky, sprawling course. The Morelands has plenty of elevation changes on fairways and greens plus deep bunkers, rolling hills, and well-placed sand bunkers. Parkland, meanwhile, sits deep in the woods with bunkers surrounding large greens, which are challenging when you finally reach them on this long layout.

(The Legends Resort cont'd)

Yardage: Heathland, 5,060 to 6,785; Moreland, 4,905 to 6,799; Parkland, 5,570 to 7,170

Par: Heathland, 71; Morelands and Parkland, 72

Open: Year-round

Tee times: Up to 6 months in advance

Green fees: $53 to $104, including cart

Facility includes: Clubhouse, pro shop, 30-acre practice facility with driving range, putting green, and chipping area, golf academy, restaurant, snack bar

Packages with resort and deals to play with other area hotels and courses.

The Long Bay Club
350 Foxhill Drive, Longs, SC 29568
800-344-5590 tee times
803-399-2222
Resort

Several waste-area holes with a lot of sand, plenty of bunkers, and small, undulating, well-bunkered greens define the 18 holes at the Long Bay Club—which, as the name would indicate, is quite long. The course is just north of Myrtle Beach.

Yardage: 5,598 to 7,021 / 4 sets of tees

Par: 72

Open: Year-round

Tee times: Up to 1 year in advance

Green fees: $65, including cart

Facility includes: Clubhouse, pro shop, driving range, chipping area, sand practice area, putting green, restaurant, snack bar

Packages with on-premise Litchfield Hotel and other area resorts.

New York City

New York City

It might be surprising that New York City has several golf courses. There are 14, although none are in Manhattan, where the closest you can get is the Chelsea Piers golf range along the Hudson River. Although most of the city courses are pleasant and provide solid golf, the wait can be very long, prompting players to head in one of three directions—west to Jersey, north to Westchester, or east to Long Island. Whichever direction you choose, it's strongly advised that you plan ahead and give yourself extra time to deal with traffic. Late afternoon weekday play during the spring or fall can sometimes be your best bet for getting a tee time and getting one at a lower rate. Long Island can be the toughest direction because many courses strongly favor local play.

Golf in the New York area is an eight- or nine-month season, depending on the winter. Courses are generally traditional northeastern with trees, some hills, and a little water sprinkled in.

Because many Manhattan hotels are still at a loss about what to do about golfers (most concierges will send you to the Chelsea Piers or greet your request with a blank stare), you may prefer setting up your tee times on your own. Don't be surprised if courses charge you a fee just to make a tee time. However, despite New York City's pricey reputation, the courses are generally not expensive to play, in relation to other golf markets.

Bethpage State Park Golf Courses

Bethpage State Park, 99 Quaker Meeting House Road,
Farmingdale, NY 11735
516-249-0700
Public

Five courses, featuring the highly acclaimed, award-winning, tournament-attracting Black course, are found in this state park. The Yellow course is straight, flat, and excellent for new players. The Red course has hills and a lot of doglegs and challenges mid-level players, as does the Blue with steep hills and small greens. The Green challenges your putting game in a major way, whereas the Black challenges and humbles the low handicappers in all facets of their games. Arguably the toughest in the New York metro area, this course has its share of hills, very deep fairways, and more hills.

Yardage: Yellow, 5,860 to 6,316; Red, 6,198 to 6,758; Blue, 6,213 to 6,684; Green, 5,903 to 6,267; Black, 6,556 to 7,065 / 3 sets of tees on each

Par: Yellow and Green, 71; Red, 70; Blue and Black, 71

Open: Year-round

Tee times: Up to 7 days in advance with state resident reservation Card; otherwise, up to 2 days in advance

Green fees: $11 to $30, depending on course and time of day (Yellow course played as 2 9-hole courses after 12 p.m. for $9 to $11)

Facility includes: Clubhouse, pro shop, driving range, 3 putting greens, cafeteria

Blue Hill Golf Club
285 Blue Hill Road, Pearl River, NY 10965
914-735-2094
Public

Three nines give you various options to fill your 18-hole outing on this course, which is 40 minutes north of midtown Manhattan. The Pines offers rolling hills, the Woodlands is flatter and tighter with tree-lined fairways, and the Lakeside...well, you figure it out. All three actually have ponds en route to undulating greens.

Yardage: 5,077 to 6,458 / 4 sets of tees

Par: 72

Open: Year-round

Tee times: Up to 48 hours in advance

Green fees: $29 to $39 (cart $13 extra per person)

Facility includes: Clubhouse, pro shop, chipping area, putting green, restaurant

Cherry Creek Golf Links
900 Reeves Avenue, Riverhead, NY 11901
516-369-8553
516-369-6500 tee times
Public

At the end of the Long Island Expressway is Riverhead, where you'll find this links-style, wide-open, long, windy course designed in the old Scottish style. Five water holes appear on the back nine, which also features a rare 600-yard par 6 finishing hole, ending a day on Cherry Creek in style.

Yardage: 5,756 to 6,597 / 4 sets of tees

Par: 73

Open: Year-round

Tee times: Up to 7 days in advance with $30 through reservation club; otherwise, day of play

(Cherry Creek Golf Links cont'd)

Green fees: $27 weekdays, $32 weekends (cart $26 extra)

Facility includes: Clubhouse, pro shop, driving range, putting green, restaurant

---

Colonial Springs Golf Course
1 Long Island Avenue, East Farmingdale, NY 11735
516-643-0051
Semi-Private

Pines, Valley, and Lake offer three different nines; as indicated by the names, you can play through trees, along hills, or by the water. Any combination of two will provide a solid round of 18.

Yardage: Combined up to 5,467 to 6,073 / 3 sets of tees

Par: 72

Open: April through December

Tee times: Up to 1 week in advance for Tuesday through Thursday, up to 1 day in advance for Friday through Sunday

Green fees: $49 to $80, including cart

Facility includes: Clubhouse, pro shop, driving range, two putting greens, restaurant, snack bar

---

Farmstead Golf and Country Club
88 Lawrence Road, Lafayette, NJ 07848
973-383-1666
Public

Three courses, 27 holes, make up this club, which is an hour west of New York City. The Lakeview nine requires good positioning because this tree-lined course has its share of doglegs and water. The Clubview nine is flatter, heavily tree-lined, and tougher than it looks. The Valley View is a little shorter with more hills than its neighbors. Combining any two will offer diversity for your outing.

Yardage: Up to 6,680, depending on configuration / 3 sets of tees

Par: Lakeview, 35; Clubview, 36; Valley View, 33 (combined 68 to 71)

Open: March through November

Tee times: Up to 7 days in advance, reservations required

Green fees: $27 weekdays, $55 weekends (cart $15 extra per person, $13 extra shared per person)

Facility includes: Clubhouse, pro shop, putting green, restaurant

---

Hauppauge Country Club
Veterans Memorial Highway, Hauppauge, NY 111788
516-724-7500
Semi-Private

A nice open course, Hauppauge is an hour east from downtown Manhattan and sees a lot of corporate play on weekdays and local play on weekends. There is plenty of water to maneuver around as you head for first-rate greens. A good test for the average player, Hauppauge is always well maintained.

Yardage: 5,925 to 6,525 / 3 sets of tees

Par: 72

Open: Year-round

Tee times: Up to 7 days with $10 advance fee per person, not refundable

Green fees: $55 Monday through Thursday, $60 Friday, $50 to $80 Saturday and Sunday, play after 3 p.m. only, including cart

Facility includes: Clubhouse, pro shop, driving range, 2 putting greens, restaurants, snack bar, banquet facilities

High Mountain Golf Club
845 Ewing Avenue, Franklin Lakes, NJ 07417
201-891-4653
Semi-Private

Only 30 miles west of New York City is a fun, scenic course on 150 acres in a serene setting. A fair amount of water and trees typify the layout with medium-sized, bent-grass greens. Weekends before 2 p.m. are for members only.

Yardage: 5,426 to 6,347 / 3 sets of tees

Par: 71

Open: March through December

Tee times: Up to 7 days in advance

Green fees: $34 to $44, including cart

Facility includes: Clubhouse, pro shop, driving range, chipping area, putting green, restaurant

La Tourette Golf Club
1001 Richmond Hill Road, Staten Island, NY 10306
718-225-GOLF for tee times
718-351-1889 for course information
Public

A short ferry ride or trip across the Verazzano will lead you to this long, hilly, wide-open, fun course that lets you get out your aggression and flex your muscles. The course is easily walkable and kept in top shape.

Yardage: 5,493 to 6,692 / 3 sets of tees

Par: 72

Open: Year-round

Tee times: Up to 12 days in advance

Green fees: $18.50 weekdays, $20.50 weekends with city resident card (obtainable at course); otherwise, $24.50 weekdays, $26.50 weekends (cart $25 extra weekdays, $26 extra weekends)

Facility includes: Pro shop, driving range, putting green, snack bar

---

Rock Hill Golf and Country Club
105 Clancy Road, Manorville, NY 11949
516-878-2250
Public

Just shy of 90 minutes outside of New York City, this fairly long course will offer you a peaceful setting with a lot of hills, four water holes, some sharp angles, and tough greens.

Yardage: 5,390 to 7,050 / 3 sets of tees

Par: 71/72

Open: Year-round

Tee times: Up to 7 days in advance

Green fees: $44 weekdays, $48 weekends (need reservations), including cart

Facility includes: Clubhouse, pro hop, driving range, putting green, golf school, restaurant

---

Spooky Brook Golf Course
582 Elizabeth Avenue, Somerset, NJ 08873
732-873-2242
Public

This is a wide-open, relaxing course that is perfect for the average golfer looking for a basic round. The course gets progressively tougher as you head from the front to back nine. Without traffic, Spooky Brook is about 45 minutes from New York City.

Yardage: 5,370 to 6,600 / 3 sets of tees

Par: 72/71

Open: Year-round

Tee times: Up to 24 hours in advance, $10 reservation fee

Green fees: $24 New Jersey residents, $34 others (cart $24 extra)

(Spooky Brook Golf Course cont'd)

Facility includes: Clubhouse, driving range, putting green, snack bar

Town of Oyster Bay Golf Course
#1 Southwoods Road, Woodbury, NY 11797
516-364-1180
Public

Less than an hour east of the city, Oyster Bay offers a short but very challenging, highly rated course with tight fairways, large greens (some multi-tiered), and four very tough finishing holes. The front nine is narrow, whereas the back nine opens up somewhat. The course is not easy to get on.

Yardage: 5,101 to 6,351 / 2 sets of tees

Par: 70

Open: Year-round

Tee times: First come, first serve

Green fees: $50 weekdays, $62 weekends (cart $50 extra)

Facility includes: Pro shop, driving range, putting green, restaurant

Van Courtlandt Park Golf course
Van Courtlandt Park South and Bailey Avenue, Bronx, NY 10471
718-543-4595
Public

You play this course because of the history—more than 100 years that had everyone from Babe Ruth to the Three Stooges teeing off. Smack-dab in the middle of the Bronx, Van Courtlandt is still a challenging, fun experience with some major hills, plenty of sand traps, a lot of trees, and tough greens. Despite the city location, the course is spread out—and you can even get there by subway.

Yardage: 5,421 to 6,122 / 3 sets of tees

Par: 70

Open: Year-round

Tee times: Up to 10 days in advance

Green fees: $26 weekdays, $28 weekends (cart $25 extra weekdays, $26 weekends)

Facility includes: Clubhouse, pro shop, snack bar

Orlando

Philadelphia and Eastern Pennsylvania

Phoenix/Scottsdale

Portland

Orlando

The Orlando area has several top golf courses aside from the Magic Kingdom, Epcot Center, and the movie studios. Disney offers nine holes of golf in three locations, whereas other first-rate courses provide lush sprawling layouts. Any hotel worth the logo on its towels should be able to point you in the direction of a course.

Despite the fact that it's Florida, it can get chilly in the winter because Orlando is north of the always-warm Miami Beach. The choice of courses is overwhelming, with 123 within a 45-minute drive of the downtown Orlando area. Prices vary depending on level of service and proximity to the Magic Kingdom. Courses are designed by some of the most famous golfers and architects in the world, including Arnold Palmer, Jack Nicklaus, Tom Fazio, Robert Trent Jones, Jr., and others. Here are a few of the best at a variety of price levels.

Arnold Palmer's Bay Hill Club and Lodge
9000 Bay Hill Boulevard, Orlando, FL 32819
407-876-2492
Resort

With Palmer's name on it, you know it has to be championship caliber. Only 15 miles from the Magic Kingdom, three 9-
hole courses occupy the lush resort grounds. Generous open
fairways with subtle elevation changes and a good amount of
water characterize the 27 holes. Large, undulating greens test
your putting game as well. The Challenger and Champion
courses are longer, but the shorter Charger course also has its
share of challenges.

Yardage: 5,235 to 7,250 / 5 sets of tees

Par: 72

Open: Year-round

Tee times: Up to 6 months in advance with lodge reservations only

Green fees: $175 resort packages

Facility includes: Clubhouse, pro shop, driving range,
chipping area, putting green, restaurant, snack bar

Packages with resort.

Baytree National Golf Links
8297 National Drive, Melbourne, FL 32941
407-259-9060
888-955-1234 tee times
Semi-Private

Just under an hour from Orlando sits this top-rated course,
featuring more than 70 white-sand bunkers, plenty of water,
and unique red-shale waste areas providing additional hazards on a tough but fair course. A wide range of tee areas allow for different levels of players to enjoy a challenging

round. The sprawling, scenic layout also provides a country-club feel.

Yardage: 4,803 to 7,043 / 5 sets of tees

Par: 72

Open: Year-round

Tee times: Up to 6 days in advance

Green fees: $39 weekdays, $49 weekends, including cart

Facility includes: Spacious clubhouse, pro shop, driving range, putting green, restaurant

---

Eagle Pines Golf Course
3451 Golf View Drive, Lake Buena Vista, FL 32830
407–824–2675
407–WDW–Golf
www.golf.disneyworld.com
Resort

One of the five 18-hole courses that make up the Disney golf experience, Eagle Pines features dish-shaped fairways and plenty of sand with native grass around the tough Pete Dye layout. Water also comes into play or sits nearby on nearly all of the well-designed, immaculately maintained holes.

Yardage: 4,838 to 6,772 / 4 sets of tees

Par: 72

Open: Year-round

Tee times: Up to 30 days in advance, up to 60 days in advance for Disney hotel guests, 48-hour cancellation policy

Green fees: Seasonal from $100 to $150, $90 for resort guests or Magic Kingdom club members, including cart

Facility includes: Clubhouse, pro shop, driving range, putting green, restaurant

Packages with 16 Disney World hotels.

Grand Cypress Resort
One North Hacaranda, Orlando, FL 32836
407-239-1904
Resort

Offering 45 holes, Cypress has golf for all players. The New Course is an 18-hole Scottish-links–style design with mounds, double greens, 154 pot bunkers, and a lot of wind. The slightly older North/South/East nines are more traditional Florida courses with narrow fairways, several water holes, and small greens. The LPGA plays here.

Yardage: The New Course, 5,314 to 6,773; North/South/East up to 7,000 / 3 sets of tees on New Course; 4 sets of tees on others

Par: 72 for each 18-hole configuration

Open: Year-round

Tee times: Up to 60 days in advance for guest of the hotels

Green fees: Seasonal from $100 to $140, including cart

Facility includes: Clubhouse, pro shop, driving range, chipping area, putting green, golf academy, restaurant

Works with guests of the Hyatt Regency Grand Cypress and the Grand Cypress villas.

Grenelefe Golf and Tennis Resort
3200 State Road 546, Haines City, FL 33844
813-422-7511
Semi-Private/Resort

Only 25 miles from Disney sits three resort courses encompassing water, woods, and wasteland. The South course has a lot of water but is playable for the high handicapper. The East course is long and tight and has small greens. The West course is quite long and tree-lined and features plenty of deep-faced bunkers.

Yardage: South, 5,174 to 6,869; East, 5,114 to 6,802; West, 5,398 to 7,325 / 4 sets of tees each

Par: South, 71; East and West, 72

Open: Year-round

Tee times: Up to 5 days in advance, up to $1^1/_2$ years in advance for resort guests

Green fees: Seasonal from $40 to $130, including cart

Facility includes: Clubhouse, pro shop, 2 driving ranges, putting green, restaurant

Golf packages with resort.

Hunter's Creek Golf Course
14401 Sports Club Way, Orlando, FL 32837
407-240-4653
Public

The longest course in Florida, Hunter's will test your strength while you play around bunkers and water to well-manicured tough greens. Easily accessible in Orlando, Hunter's is a popular, highly rated facility that is less expensive than the Disney courses.

Yardage: 5,755 to 7,432 / 4 sets of tees

Par: 72

Open: Year-round

Tee times: Up to 3 to 7 days in advance, seasonal

Green fees: Seasonal from $40 to $79, including cart

Facility includes: Clubhouse, pro shop, driving range, putting green, snack bar

Lake Buena Vista Golf Course
One Lake Drive, Lake Buena Vista, FL 32830
407-828-3741
407-WDW-Golf
www.golf.disneyworld.com
Resort

Hosting both PGA and LPGA events, this Disney layout is shorter than some of its counterparts, but it's no Mickey Mouse course. Plenty of pine trees, a lot of water, and small, well-bunkered greens challenge your shot-making skills.

Yardage: 5,194 to 6,819 / 4 sets of tees

Par: 73/72

Open: Year-round

Tee times: Up to 30 days in advance, up to 60 days in advance for Disney hotel guests, 48-hour cancellation policy

Green fees: Seasonal from $100 to $150, $90 for resort guests or Magic Kingdom club members, including cart

Facility includes: Clubhouse, pro shop, driving range, putting green, restaurant

Packages with 16 Disney World hotels.

Magnolia Golf Course
1950 West Magnolia Drive, Lake Buena Vista, FL 32830
407-824-2288
407-WDW-Golf
www.golf.disneyworld.com
Resort

The longest of the five Disney 18-holers at just shy of 7,200 yards, Magnolia is picturesque with some 1,500 magnolia trees. In addition to the flowers and a sixth hole with a Mickey-Mouse–shaped bunker, the course has nearly 100 more typically tough bunkers, 12 water holes, rolling fairways, and elevated tees.

Yardage: 5,253 to 7,190 / 4 sets of tees

Par: 72

Open: Year-round

Tee times: Up to 30 days in advance, up to 60 days in advance for Disney hotel guests, 48-hour cancellation policy

Green fees: Seasonal from $100 to $150, $90 for resort guests or Magic Kingdom club members, including cart

Facility includes: Clubhouse, pro shop, driving range, putting green, restaurant

Packages with 16 Disney World hotels.

Osprey Ridge Golf Course
3451 Golf View Drive, Lake Buena Vista, FL 32830
407-824-2675
407-WDW-Golf
www.golf.disneyworld.com
Resort

Another Disney gem, Osprey is a highly rated new Fazio course featuring plenty of sand, water, and mounds. Playing along a meandering ridge with rolling fairways through the tropical wilderness, you'll encounter many elevation changes and a lot of hazards on route to large greens.

Yardage: 5,402 to 7,101 / 4 sets of tees

Par: 72

Open: Year-round

Tee times: Up to 30 days in advance, up to 60 days in advance for Disney hotel guests, 48-hour cancellation policy

Green fees: Seasonal from $100 to $150, $90 for resort guests or Magic Kingdom club members, including cart

Facility includes: Clubhouse, pro shop, driving range, putting green, restaurant

Packages with 16 Disney World hotels.

Palm Golf Course
1950 Magnolia Drive, Lake Buena Vista 32830
407-824-2288
407-WDW-Golf
www.golf.disneyworld.com
Resort

Along with Magnolia, Palm is one of the two original Disney World courses. The course is a woodlands-style layout with a lot of water and sand plus some interesting par 3s. Several lakes test your accuracy and provide a scenic backdrop for this, perhaps the most forgiving of the Disney five.

Yardage: 5,311 to 6,957 / 4 sets of tees

Par: 72

Open: Year-round

Tee times: Up to 30 days in advance, up to 60 days in advance for Disney hotel guests, 48-hour cancellation policy

Green fees: Seasonal from $100 to $150, $90 for resort guests or Magic Kingdom club members, including cart

Facility includes: Clubhouse, pro shop, driving range, putting green, restaurant

Packages with 16 Disney World hotels.

Tournament Players Club at Sawgrass
110 TPC Boulevard, Ponte Vedra Beach, FL 32082
904-273-3235
Resort

Not actually in the Orlando vicinity, about two-and-a-half hours away, this prestigious golf facility can't be left out. Famous for the Stadium course, there are actually two 18-hole championship courses on the facility. The Valley course sees less activity than its well-known neighbor but is a good test with a lot of water, some trees, and Bermuda grass greens. The highly ranked Stadium course has less water in play, although it does have the famous 17th hole with its island green. The trees come into play on this tighter, magnificently designed layout, which also sports Bermuda grass greens. TPC is 15 miles from Jacksonville in Northern Florida.

Yardage: Stadium 5,000 to 6,937; Valley 5,126 to 6,864 / 4 to 6 sets of tees on each

Par: 72

Open: Year-round

Tee times: Up to 30 days in advance for Marriott resort guests

Green fees: Stadium from $105 to $135 (cart $24 extra per person); Valley seasonal from $75 to $95 (cart $24 extra per person)

Facility includes: Clubhouse, pro shop, driving range, chipping area, putting green, restaurant, snack bar

Packages with resort.

Philadelphia and Eastern Pennsylvania

Phillie offers courses that suit every skill level at a range of prices. From Cobbs Creek in the heart of the historic city to courses in Hershey, there are first-rate layouts sprinkled generously throughout the area. The Philadelphia Convention and Visitors Bureau is helpful as are some of the major area hotels.

Courses are primarily traditional with trees and some water. As is the case with most northeastern cities, the limited city space means you'll find more sprawling layouts with more amenities outside of town, so you might prefer making your own arrangements. Although avid players will try to make golf a year-round pastime, it's primarily a nine-month activity in the City of Brotherly Love.

Blackwood Golf Course
510 Red Corner Road, Douglassville, PA 19518
610-385-6200
Public

A fairly open, relatively short course, Blackwood is challenging, forcing you to hit over two ponds on your way to bent-grass, often undulating greens. The fun layout sits on the outskirts of Reading.

Yardage: 4,826 to 6,400 / 3 sets of tees

Par: 70

Open: Year-round

Tee times: Up to 13 days in advance for weekends, first come, first serve on weekdays

Green fees: $ 17 weekdays, $ 28 weekends (cart $21.50 extra)

Facility includes: Clubhouse, pro shop, driving range, putting green, snack bar

Buena Vista Country Club
P.O. Box 307, Buena, NJ 08310
609-697-3733
Public

Midway between Philadelphia and Atlantic City (about 30 minutes from each) is a long, tight course with tree-lined fairways throughout. Between the trees and the sand, you're forced to hit the ball straight or lose it. Greens are fast on this challenging course.

Yardage: 5,641 to 6,869 / 4 sets of tees

Par: 72

Open: Year-round

Tee times: Up to 5 days in advance

Green fees: $27 weekdays, $34 weekends (cart $14 extra per person)

Facility includes: Clubhouse, pro shop, driving range, chipping area, putting green, restaurant and banquet facility, snack bar

---

Cobb's Creek Golf Course
72nd Street and Lansdowne Avenue, Philadelphia, PA 19151
215-877-8707
Public

If you like hitting over water, you'll have fun here as the course plays around and over a meandering creek with six shots over water on the first four holes. The first nine are tight, but the second nine open up a bit more. The accessible course is popular with local golfers.

Yardage: 6,130 to 6,606 / 3 sets of tees

Par: 71

Open: Year-round

Tee times: Up to 7 days in advance for weekends, first come, first serve for weekdays

Green fees: $22 weekdays, $26 weekends (cart $12.85 extra per person)

Facility includes: Clubhouse, pro shop, driving range, 2 putting greens, snack bar

---

Country Club of Hershey
1000 East Derry Road, Hershey, PA 17033
717-533-2360
Resort

In the midst of chocolate country sit three excellent courses: two resort and one public. The East course, which hosts the Nike Hershey Open, is a long, wide-open course with a fair amount of water leading to elevated greens. The West course is a shorter, tighter layout with more character and a rich history, including PGA and LPGA events. Old trees and fast greens highlight this majestic old course. Down the road, the

(Country Club of Hershey cont'd)

South course (formerly Hershey Parkview) is a public facility that plays around a creek, which comes into play on several holes. A well-manicured, tight course with good placement is the name of the game on the South course, which plays longer than its yardage.

Yardage: East, 5,646 to 7,060; West, 5,900 to 6,800; South, 4,856 to 6,204 / 3 sets of tees on each

Par: East, 71; West, 73; South, 71/70

Open: Year-round

Tee times: East and West when making room reservations at resort; South up to 7 days in advance

Green fees: East, $85; West, $110; South, $39 Monday through Thursday, $47 Friday through Sunday, including cart

Facility includes: Pro shops, clubhouses, driving range, putting green, restaurants, snack bars

*Packages with Country Club, Hershey Hotel,
and Hershey Lodge.*

Country Club at Woodloch Springs
One Woodloch Drive, Hawley, PA 18428
717-685-2100
Resort

Just over two hours from Phillie and an hour from Scranton sits an out-of-the-way resort-only course. The hilly layout is tight and plays along a mountainside with several ponds leading to bent-grass greens.

Yardage: 4,973 to 6,579 / 3 sets of tees

Par: 72

Open: Year-round

Tee times: Up to 10 days in advance

Green fees: $60 weekdays, $75 weekends, including cart

Facility includes: Clubhouse, pro shop, driving range, putting green, restaurant and grill

Eagle Lodge Country Club
Ridge and Manor Roads, Lafayette Hills, PA 19444
610-825-9198
Resort/Public

East Lodge features a long, tough, and extremely hilly top-rated resort course. The layout includes long par 3s en route to well-maintained, very large greens. One of the closest resorts to the city, the country club is 25 minutes from downtown.

Yardage: 5,260 to 6,700 / 3 sets of tees

Par: 71

Open: Year-round

Tee times: Up to 7 days in advance

Green fees: $80, including cart

Facility includes: Clubhouse, pro shop, driving range, putting green, grill and banquet facility

Resort golf packages.

General Washington Golf Course
2750 Egypt Road, Audubon, PA 19403
612-666-7602
Public

No, George Washington didn't sleep here, but the course is only 10 minutes from Valley Forge. (It's also 10 minutes from Phillie.) Part of a large recreation center, G.W. is carved out of the woods and is tight in spots. The popular 50-year-old course isn't particularly long but has several challenges with three ponds coming into play and multi-tiered greens.

Yardage: 5,325 to 6,402 / 3 sets of tees

Par: 71/72

(General Washington Golf Course cont'd)

Open: Year-round

Tee times: Up to 7 days in advance

Green fees: $19 to $38, depending on day and time of day, including cart in morning ($11 cart fee later in the day)

Facility includes: Clubhouse, pro shop, short driving range (150 yards), restaurant and banquet facilities, ice skating rink

---

Royal Oaks Golf Course
3350 West Oak Street, Lebanon, PA 17042
717-274-2212
Public

About 90 minutes from Phillie and 20 minutes from Hershey is a highly ranked, fairly new course that is often compared to the finer designs at Myrtle Beach. The lush links at Royal Oaks offer several spectacular holes in a sprawling wide-open layout with many mounds and a lot of water coming into play on the back nine.

Yardage: 4,800 to 6,730 / 5 sets of tees

Par: 71

Open: Year-round

Tee times: Up to 7 days in advance without credit card, longer with a credit card

Green fees: $20 weekday to walk, $27 to ride, $50 weekend, including cart

Facility includes: Clubhouse, pro shop, driving range, chipping area, putting green, restaurant, snack bar

*Inquire about packages with Hotel Hershey
and Quality Inn.*

Upper Perk Golf Course
2324 Ott Road, Pennsburg, PA 18073
215-679-5594
Public

This busy course is just over an hour from downtown and features a lot of trees and five water holes. The layout is flat on the first nine and has rolling hills on the back. The walkable course is well maintained from tees to spacious greens.

Yardage: 5,249 to 6,381 / 3 sets of tees

Par: 71

Open: Year-round

Tee times: Up to 7 days in advance for weekdays, up to 14 days in advance for weekends

Green fees: $18 weekdays, $29 weekends (cart $10 extra per person)

Facility includes: Clubhouse, pro shop, putting green, snack bar

Wyncote Golf Club
50 Wyncote Drive, Oxford, PA 19363
610-965-GOLF
Semi-Private

If you can't get to Scotland, go to Oxford, Pennsylvania. This unique inland links course is a traditional Scottish-links layout complete with mounds and wind. The beautiful long layout sits an hour from the Liberty Bell and provides numerous twists and turns on meticulous fairways.

Yardage: 5,454 to 7,010 / 4 sets of tees

Par: 72

Open: Year-round

Tee times: Up to 7 days in advance

(Wyncote Golf Club cont'd)

Green fees: $50 weekdays (cart $15 extra per person), $80 weekends, including cart

Facility includes: Clubhouse, pro shop, driving range, chipping area, putting green, snack bar

Phoenix/Scottsdale

Courses in the Phoenix/Scottsdale area are, as one might expect, primarily the desert variety, with picturesque backdrops and plenty of sand. Narrow fairways with little room for error lead to the target golf label on many of the area courses. More recently, diverse courses such as the Raven have sprung up among the 160 places to play that are scattered across the Phoenix landscape.

Visitors can play more than 100 courses that are either resort or public facilities. Peak season for golf falls between January and May, with shoulder seasons in the spring and fall. The summer off season will find lower rates but higher temperatures, making it almost impossible to endure a comfortable round of 18 holes.

Most of the major-name downtown Phoenix hotels plus those properties in the Scottsdale Resort Corridor will assist you in setting up your advance tee times. The shoulder season (between the extremely hot summer off season and the popular playing winter) is often the prime time for visitors, because there is slightly less on-course traffic and it is easier to attain the tee time you want. For rooms and tee time reservations, including more than 30 area courses, Tee Time Travel, 800-827-3456, is one of the popular golf-packaging services. If you call courses or hotels, ask about the Mesa Golf package, which offers packages with numerous area hotels.

The Boulders Resort
34831 Tom Darlington Drive, Carefree, AZ 85377
800-595-1717
602-488-9028
Resort/Public

The Boulders has two marvelous high-end resort courses. The North features generous tee shots into wide-landing areas with plenty of desert around to test your accuracy. The South course plays around rock formations and boulders. Both courses feature Bermuda fairways and bent-grass greens and spectacular scenery, and guests receive plenty of amenities. The Boulders is just north of Scottsdale and 33 miles from the Phoenix Sky Harbor airport.

Yardage: North, 4,893 to 6,731; South, 4,715 to 6,589 / 4 sets of tees

Par: North, 72; South, 71

Open: Year-round

Tee times: Up to 1 year in advance for guests, depending on availability for non-guests

Green fees: Seasonal from $75 to $200, including cart

Facility includes: Clubhouse, pro shop, driving range, chipping area, putting green, restaurant

Resort packages include unlimited golf, spa, and more.

Kierland Golf Club
15636 Clubgate Drive, Scottsdale, AZ 85254
602-922-9283
Public

This 27-hole layout can be played in any of three 9-hole configurations to complete a challenging 18-hole card. The lush courses feature rolling hills, emerald fairways, several varieties of lush grass, and striking elevation changes, with one of the three ninth holes dropping 80 feet from tee to green. All

(Kierland Golf Club cont'd)

three courses play around three lakes and use many of the 300 bunkers strategically placed on the wide-open park-like setting.

Just over 30 minutes from the Phoenix/Scottsdale airport, the course will soon boast a neighboring 700-room resort hotel due to open in early 2000.

Yardage: 4,691 to 6,900, depending on configuration and tee area / 4 sets of tees

Par: 72

Open: Year-round

Tee times: Up to 30 days in advance

Green fees: Seasonal from $45 to $125, including cart

Facility includes: Clubhouse, pro shop, driving range, chipping area, putting green, snack bar

---

Marriott's Camelback Golf Club
7847 North Mockingbird Lane, Scottsdale, AZ 85253
602-948-6770
800-242-2635
Resort/Public

The two courses on Camelback include Indian Bend and Padre. Indian Bend is a unique American links-style course (non-desert) that plays long and is open with some water. Padre is narrow and well bunkered with various types of trees and elevated greens. In the heart of Scottsdale, these courses are popular, and the service and amenities are first rate.

Yardage: Indian Bend, 5,917 to 7,014; Padre, 5,586 to 6,559 / 3 sets of tees

Par: Indian Bend, 72; Padre, 72/71

Open: Year-round

Tee times: Up to 30 days in advance for guests, up to 7 days in advance for non-guests

Green fees: Seasonal $35 to $115, including cart

Facility includes: Clubhouse, pro shop, driving range, chipping area, putting green, restaurant, snack bar

Guests can arrange to also play on other local Marriott properties.

Ocotillo Golf Club
3752 South Clubhouse Drive, Chandler, AZ 85248
602-917-6660
Public

For those who think Arizona is dry, this highly rated course, only 30 minutes from Phoenix, is the place to play. Winding around several lakes and cascading waterfalls, Ocotillo defies you to play an accurate game or has you fishing balls from the water. The 27 holes flow smoothly, and, well-maintained, flowing fairways complement the water hazards nicely. Although the White course is better suited for long hitters, the Blue is shorter but sports more water hazards. The Gold mixes up the short and long par 4s and is preferred by newer players.

Yardage: 6,533 to 6,729, depending on configuration and tee area / 4 sets of tees

Par: 71/72, depending on configuration

Open: Year-round

Tee times: Up to 30 days in advance

Green fees: Seasonal from $45 to $115, including cart

Facility includes: Clubhouse, pro shop, driving range, restaurant

Golf packages with The Pointe at South Mountain and various other area hotels.

The Phoenician Golf Club
6000 East Camelback Road, Scottsdale, AZ 85251
800-888-8234
602-423-2449
Resort

Three nines make up this lavish upscale course. The Oasis puts you in the tropics with plenty of water amid beautiful scenery. The Desert is desert golf with some elevation changes, and the Canyon plays through a canyon with some marvelous views of downtown Phoenix. All three courses are in excellent shape and feature bent-grass fairways. This is golf in the lap of luxury—and only nine miles from the Phoenix/Scottsdale airport for those on the run.

Yardage: 4,470 to 6,310 / 4 sets of tees

Par: 72

Open: Year-round

Tee times: Up to 30 days in advance, up to 60 days in advance for resort guests

Green fees: Seasonal from $140 to $170, including cart

Facility includes: Clubhouse, pro shop, driving range, chipping area, putting green, restaurant, snack bar

Discount rates and packages.

The Raven
3636 East Baseline Road, Phoenix, AZ 85040
602-243-3636
Public

Undulating greens, crystal clear lakes, and the South Mountains as a spectacular backdrop are only part of the first-rate Raven's special lure. The course also sports 6,000 pine trees in the middle of Arizona, something you don't see every day. A mix of long and short par 4s provide opportunities for long hitters to show their muscle and finesse players to excel at the short game. Multi-tiered greens, well-placed bunkers, two lake holes, and some very tricky par 3s create a course that requires careful strategy.

Yardage: 7,000 from back tees / 4 sets of tees

Par: 72

Open: Year-round

Tee times: Up to 90 days in advance

Green fees: Seasonal from $65 to $145, including cart

Facility includes: Clubhouse, pro shop, driving range, restaurant, two snack bars

Some hotels offer vouchers for course discounts with stay; most will book tee times

Sedona Golf Resort
35 Ridge Trail Drive, Sedona, AZ 86351
602-284-9355
Public

Nearly two hours north of the Phoenix/Scottsdale area, Sedona is worth the trip. One of the most scenic courses in the world makes it almost hard to concentrate on your game. More than 80 bunkers, five lakes, tree-lined fairways, and some tricky greens make the course challenging for players at a variety of levels. Sedona also provides a rare opportunity to play golf at an elevation of 4,000 feet and smack a few long shots.

Yardage: 5,059 to 6,640 / 4 sets of tees

Par: 71

Open: Year-round

Tee times: Up to 14 days in advance, up to 30 days in advance for resort guests

Green fees: $84 weekdays, $94 weekends, including cart

Facility includes: Clubhouse, pro shop, driving range, instruction available, restaurant

New Resort Golf and Conference Center offers golf packages.

Sheraton San Marcos Resort
100 North Dakota Street, Chandler, AZ
602-963-3358
Resort/Public

Just 30 miles from Phoenix, this resort is highly rated, following a $19 million facelift. The course is tree-lined with canals and ponds running through it, which make it both challenging and scenic. It's not desert golf for those who appreciate the variety—and some shade. Sheraton San Marcos is only 30 minutes from Phoenix International Airport.

Yardage: 5,431 to 6,541 / 3 sets of tees

Par: 73/72

Open: Year-round

Tee times: Up to 7 days in advance, up to 1 year in advance for hotel guests

Green fees: Seasonal from $22 to $95, including cart

Facility includes: Clubhouse, pro shop, driving range, chipping area, putting green, restaurant

Resort packages offered.

Stonecreek Golf Club
4435 East Paradise Village Parkway South,
Paradise Valley, AZ 85032
602-953-9111
800-GOTRY18 tee times
Semi-Private

A links-style course, Stonecreek insists you keep the ball on the fairway. Rolling hills and a winding creek blend into the well-laid-out 10-year-old course, which sits smack dab in the middle of the Phoenix/Scottsdale area and will sport a brand new neighboring Embassy Suites by late 1999.

Yardage: 5,018 to 6,871 / 4 sets of tees

Par: 71

Open: Year-round

Tee times: Up to 60 days in advance

Green fees: Seasonal from $40 to $130, including cart

Facility includes: Clubhouse, top-rated pro shop, driving range, putting green, restaurant

Discount packages with several area hotels and upcoming tie-ins with Embassy Suites.

SunRidge Canyon Golf Club
13100 North SunRidge Drive, Fountain Hills, AZ 85268
602-837-5100
Public

This new 18-hole gem is just east of Scottsdale and is easily accessible from all local resorts. Wide generous fairways are inviting, but the twists and subtle shifts in landscape make the layout quite challenging. Unlike most courses where fairways run parallel to each other, SunRidge has 18 holes in a continuous loop, descending through one canyon and ascending through another. Besides first-rate golf, the course provides breathtaking mountain views, so pack a camera in your bag.

Yardage: 5,141 to 6,822 / 4 sets of tees

Par: 71

Open: Year-round

Tee times: Up to 30 days in advance

Green fees: Seasonal from $65 to $165, including cart

Facility includes: Clubhouse, pro shop, driving range, short-game practice area, dining room

Hotels can arrange tee times.

Superstition Springs Golf Club
6542 Baseline Road, Mesa, AZ 85206
602-985-5622
800-468-7918
Public

This magnificent, highly-rated course combines a links-style setting with a traditional layout. Rolling hills, a dozen water holes and a spectacular finishing hole are among the highlights of this well-crafted course, which sits just 20 miles from Phoenix.

Yardage: 5,328 to 7,005 / 3 sets of tees

Par: 72

Open: Year-round

Tee times: Up to 7 days, up to 60 days with reservation fee

Green fees: Seasonal from $40 to $120, including cart

Facility includes: Driving range, chipping area, putting green, pro shop, restaurant, banquet facilities, golf school

Packages available with area resorts.

Tournament Players Club of Scottsdale
17020 North Hayden Road, Scottsdale, AZ 85255
602-585-7309
Resort/Public

Home of the PGA Phoenix Open, this is one of the only stadium courses that allows the public to step up to the tees where the pros play. Lush fairways, fast (often tricky) greens, 72 bunkers, lakes, an island green on the 501-yard 15th hole, and a host of other challenges make the course enticing, yet within the grasp of a low handicapper. The neighboring Desert course is shorter and tighter than the Stadium course, forcing you to put your emphasis on accuracy and play target golf (to avoid desert areas) until you reach more generous greens.

Yardage: Desert, 4,715 to 6,552; Stadium, 5,567 to 6,992 / 4 sets of tees each

Par: 71

Open: Year-round

Tee times: Desert, up to 7 days in advance; Stadium, up to 90 days in advance

Green fees: Stadium, seasonal from $67 to $160; Desert, seasonal from $35 to $44, including cart

Facility includes: Pro shop, state-of-the-art practice facilities, restaurants

Package deals with neighboring Scottsdale Princess Resort.

Troon North Golf Club
10320 East Dynamite Boulevard, North Scottsdale, AZ 85255
602-585-5300
Semi-Private

Troon has two outstanding courses that offer long target golf with elevation changes as they play through cactus, boulders, and desert plants indigenous to the region. At 3,000 feet above sea level, you'll feel like a power hitter. The Monument Course features wide fairways and is more forgiving than the neighboring Pinnacle, with slightly tighter fairways and smaller greens. Although the Pinnacle is the more scenic of the two, both are consistently rated among the top in the state. Troon is 50 minutes from downtown Phoenix and 30 minutes from Scottsdale.

Yardage: Monument, 5,050 to 7,028; Pinnacle, 4,980 to 7,044 / 5 sets of tees on each

Par: 72

Open: Year-round

Tee times: Up to 5 days in advance, up to 30 days in advance for 2 to 15 with 30-day advance fee of $20 per player

(Troon North Golf Club cont'd)

Green fees: Seasonal from $75 to $180, including cart

Facility includes: Clubhouse, pro shop, driving range, chipping area, putting green, grill, snack bar

Resort suites arrange tee times.

Wigwam Resort
300 Wigwam Boulevard, Litchfield Park, AZ 85340
602-935-3811
Resort/Public

Adjacent to the 65-year-old, highly acclaimed Wigwam Resort Hotel sit three sprawling courses amid a 463-acre oasis. The long Gold course is a challenge for big hitters, featuring a 605-yard par 5 10th hole plus plenty of sand traps and elevated greens throughout. The Blue course is shorter, nicely laid out, and kinder to newer players. The Red course, although newer than the others, has an old-fashioned layout with plenty of challenges amid lush surrounding. The popular conference facility is 20 minutes from Phoenix.

Yardage: Gold, 5,821 to 6,867; Blue, 5,235 to 6,130; Red, 5,821 to 6,867 / 4 sets of tees

Par: Gold, 72; Blue, 70; Red, 72

Open: Year-round

Tee times: Up to 5 days in advance, up to 6 months in advance for hotel guests

Green fees: Seasonal from $27 to $95, including cart

Facility includes: Clubhouse, pro shop, 2 driving ranges, putting green, restaurant

Golf packages include unlimited play, club storage, airport transportation, and so on.

Portland

Portland, like the rest of the country, is feeling the golf boom, and courses are being built at a rapid rate. Courses, many along the coastline, run the gamut from tree-lined to sandy to wide open, and most have marvelous views. In an ecology state, the courses work hard to stay within the parameters of ecology and preservation. A lot of courses have wildlife and wetlands surrounding them.

Courses are open and playable year-round because the city gets some rain in the winter but not as much snow as one might expect; it sits in a banana belt with the neighboring mountains taking the brunt of the winter.

Pumpkin Ridge is probably the best known in the area, and it's one of many public facilities within a short drive from downtown. Hotel concierge desks can make arrangements at most courses; many concierges have relationships with the courses to best insure that their guests get good tee times. They can also help with transportation and directions.

You can call the four municipal Portland courses at a central number, 503-289-1818. Oregon Tourism, 503-986-0000, publishes a golf directory in the event you want to reach other locations in the state.

Broadmoor Golf Course
3509 North East Columbia Boulevard, Portland, OR 97211
503-281-1337
Public

Between downtown Portland and the airport is Broadmoor, a mature (nearly 70 years old), beautifully landscaped course that is tight, tree-lined, and challenging. Some water and enough bunkers keep you planning your next shot carefully.

Yardage: 5,384 to 6,467 / 3 sets of tees

Par: 74/72

Open: Year-round

(Broadmoor Golf Course cont'd)

Tee times: Prior Monday for the following 2 weeks

Green fees: $20 weekdays, $22 weekends (cart $11 extra per person)

Facility includes: Clubhouse, pro shop, driving range, putting green, restaurant and lounge

---

Eastmoreland Golf Course
2425 South East Bybee Boulevard, Portland, OR 97202
503-775-2900
503-292-8270
Public

Only seven minutes from downtown, this scenic course plays around Crystal Springs Lake. Tight fairways and a lot of water characterize this excellent layout. The course is popular but very well maintained considering the traffic.

Yardage: 5,646 to 6,529 / 3 sets of tees

Par: 72

Open: Year-round

Tee times: Up to 7 days in advance in person, up to 6 days in advance by phone

Green fees: $19 weekdays, $21 weekends (cart $25 extra)

Facility includes: Clubhouse, pro shop, driving range, chipping area, putting green, restaurant and banquet facility

Tee times from downtown hotels.

Glendoveer Golf Course
1415 North East Glisan Street, Portland, OR 97230
503-292-8570 tee times
503-253-7507
Public

Glendoveer is only 15 minutes from downtown and incorporates hills, water, trees, and all the usual on-course challenges.

The East course offers easier fun, but the shorter West course is for newer or higher-handicap players. Both old courses are easily walkable and kept in good condition.

Yardage: East, 5,142 to 6,296; West, 5,117 to 5,922 / 3 sets of tees

Par: East, 75/73; West, 75/71

Open: Year-round

Tee times: Up to 7 days in advance in person, up to 6 days in advance by phone

Green fees: $19 weekdays, $21 weekends (cart $24 extra)

Facility includes: Clubhouse, pro shop, driving range, chipping area, putting green, restaurant

Heron Lakes Golf Course

3500 North Victory Boulevard, Portland, OR 97217

503-289-1818

Public

Two highly rated courses provide two styles of the same game. The Great Blue course is links style with 187 bunkers and water everywhere. This challenging course makes you pull out every club in your bag. The neighboring Greenback is quite green with tree-lined fairways that encourage you not to stray. Plenty of water and a lot of birds round out the scenic, slightly shorter course.

Yardage: Great Blue, 5,142 to 6,324; Greenback, 5,224 to 6,595 / 4 sets of tees on Great Blue; 3 sets of tees on Greenback

Par: 72

Open: Year-round

Tee times: Up to 7 days in advance in person, up to 6 days in advance by phone

Green fees: Great Blue, $31; Greenback; $19 weekdays, $21 weekends (cart $25 extra)

(Heron Lakes Golf Course cont'd)

Facility includes: Clubhouse, pro shop, driving range, chipping area, putting green, restaurant

Packages with Doubletree Inn.

Langdon Farms Golf Club
24377 North East Airport Road, Aurora, OR 97002
503-678-4653
Public

A farm theme makes Langdon a unique experience. Only 20 minutes from downtown, this is a long links-style course with depressed fairways, plenty of mounds, and bent-grass greens. The new course is rapidly growing in popularity.

Yardage: 5,249 to 6,935 / 4 sets of tees

Par: 71

Open: Year-round

Tee times: Up to 60 days in advance

Green fees: $55 to $70, including cart

Facility includes: Farmhouse clubhouse, pro shop, driving range, putting course with sand traps, restaurant

Discount card program available.

Pumpkin Ridge Golf Club
12930 NW Old Pumpkin Ridge Road, Cornelious, OR 97113
503-647-9977
Semi-Private

One of the top-rated public courses in the country, Pumpkin Ridge's Ghost Creek course is a must for any serious golfer. This modern classic links-style course has holes that were sculpted individually and play around a meandering creek, which runs through all but four of them. With bent grass from tees to greens, the course is very tough but fair, and it rewards good shots. Pumpkin Ridge is also home to a private course. Pumpkin Ridge is 30 minutes west of Portland.

Yardage: 5,326 to 6,839 / 4 sets of tees

Par: 71

Open: Year-round

Tee times: Up to 50 days in advance, with $10 per person advance reservation fee

Green fees: Seasonal from $75 to $110 (cart $15 extra per person)

Facility includes: Clubhouse, pro shop, driving range, chipping area, putting green, golf school, grill

---

The Resort at the Mountain
68010 East Fairway Avenue, Welches, OR 97067
800-669-4653
Resort/Public

The resort offers an excellent layout in the valley below. The course is narrow with a wide variety of holes to keep you guessing. It's worth the nearly one-hour drive from Portland, and the course sees a lot of business activity.

Yardage: 5,200 to 6,700 / 4 sets of tees

Par: 72/70

Open: Year-round

Tee times: Up to 14 days in advance, guests can book a tee time when making reservations at the resort.

Green fees: $32 weekdays, $40 weekends (carts $26 extra)

Facility includes: Clubhouse, pro shop, shipping area, putting green, restaurant

Packages available.

Salem Golf Club
2025 Golf Course Road, Salem, OR 97302
503-363-6652
Public

(Salem Golf Club cont'd)

A visit to nearby Salem lets you play this popular course, which is ideal if you like big trees because there are a lot of them lining the fairways. Set in a park, this classic gem offers a pleasant, relaxing escape into the country.

Yardage: 5,163 to 6,200 / 3 sets of tees

Par: 72

Open: Year-round

Tee times: Up to 3 days in advance for weekends, prior Monday for weekends

Green fees: $35 (carts $20 extra)

Facility includes: Clubhouse, award-winning pro shop, driving range, chipping area, putting green, restaurant

---

Salishan Golf Links
Highway 101, Gleneden Beach, OR 97388
800-890-0387
Resort/Public

An hour from Salem and just over two hours from Portland is a marvelous seaside course and resort just outside Lincoln City. Ocean breezes can play havoc on this seaside course, so take the wind into consideration while playing this tough, links-style layout.

Yardage: 5,389 to 6,453 / 3 sets of tees

Par: 72

Open: Year-round

Tee times: Up to 14 days in advance, up to 1 year in advance for guests

Green fees: Seasonal from $25 to $50 (cart $25 extra)

Facility includes: Clubhouse, pro shop, driving range, chipping areas, putting course, putting green, restaurant

Ask about resort packages.

St. Louis

Salt Lake City

San Antonio

San Diego

San Francisco and Northern California

Seattle/Tacoma

St. Louis

You can find a number of excellent courses a short distance outside the city itself. From the arch, you can see several of the 111 public facilities of the St. Louis area, which spills into neighboring Illinois. Courses are mostly tree-lined with large oaks, blue grass fairways, and bent-grass greens. Although new facilities continue to open regularly, other courses date back as far as 1901. Many major tournaments have been held in the city, and legends of the game such as Hale Irwin make the city their home base.

Although there is no central source for booking tee times (you're on your own), you can find *The Golf Directory of St. Louis Area Golf Courses* at golf shops and local bookstores.

This guide details the golf in the area and further assists you to hit the greens. Plan to play between March and November when the weather is accommodating. Don't worry about running up major expenses because the highest-end area courses just exceed $100.

Annbriar Golf Course
1524 Birdie Lane, Waterloo, MO 62298
888-939-5191
618-939-4653
Public

Thirty minutes from downtown, Annbriar is one of the area's premier courses. The outstanding layout has a bit of everything for all levels of golfers. The links-style front nine has plenty of mounds with generous landing areas. The back nine is tight, hilly, and heavily wooded. Your choice of seven—that's right, seven—tee boxes allows you to play the course short, long, or anywhere in between.

Yardage: 4,792 to 6,841 / 5 to 7 sets of tees

Par: 72

Open: Year-round

Tee times: Up to 7 days in advance

Green fees: $48 Monday through Thursday, $58 Friday through Sunday, including cart

Facility includes: Clubhouse, pro shop, driving range, 2 putting greens, restaurant, banquet facility, snack bar

Cherry Hills Golf Course
16700 Manchester Road, Grover, MO 63040
314-458-4133
Public

Plenty of trees, some water, and a lot of bunkers make this former country-club course challenging. Playing along rolling hills, the 25-year-old scenic layout is only 12 miles from downtown St. Louis.

Yardage: 5,359 to 6,389 / 3 sets of tees

Par: 71

Open: Year-round

Tee times: Up to 7 days in advance

Green fees: $49 weekdays, $55 Friday through Sunday, including cart

Facility includes: Clubhouse, pro shop, driving range, putting green, cart valets, restaurant, banquet facility

Eagle Springs Golf Course
2575 Redman Road, St. Louis, MO 63136
314-355-7277
Public

A fun course, Eagle Springs is good for all player levels. Rolling hills, tree-lined fairways, several lakes, and a winding creek will test your game as you aim for bent-grass greens. Eagle Springs is accessible—in the city itself—and is popular, so plan ahead.

Yardage: 5,453 to 6,454 / 3 sets of tees

Par: 72

Open: Year-round

Tee times: Up to 5 days in advance

Green fees: $30 weekdays, $39 weekends, including cart

Facility includes: Clubhouse, pro shop, driving range, putting green, par 3 9-hole course, snack bar

Gateway National Golf Links
18 Golf Drive, Madison IL 62060
314-421-4653
Public

The brand new Gateway National is built on an 1890 cattle stockyard in East St. Louis. Adjacent to Grand National Racetrack and a chip shot from the famed arch, the course sports

(Gateway National Golf Links cont'd)

huge sweeping mounds that look like dunes and flank a burn (creek) that slashes through the course, requiring a significant amount of strategy. Sitting on 220 acres, the course has a high-end feel with reasonable green fees and great views of downtown St. Louis.

Yardage: 5,200 to 7,300 / 5 sets of tees

Par: 71

Open: Year-round

Tee times: Up to 7 days in advance, up to 8 days in advance or more for $75 prepayment rate, including cart

Green fees: $45 weekdays, $48 weekends (carts $5 extra per person)

Facility includes: Clubhouse, pro shop, driving range, putting green, restaurant, snack bar

Local and downtown hotels can arrange advance tee times.

Hawk Ridge Golf Course
18 Hawk Ridge Drive, Lake Saint Louis, MO 63366
314-561-2828
Public

Hawk Ridge offers a little of everything from links-style holes with rolling hills to some tighter wooded holes in a tough but fair layout. Tall-grass rough, plenty of water, and bunkers are all part of this fairly new, scenic course that sits an hour west of St. Louis. Birds and wildlife are in abundance.

Yardage: 4,883 to 6,619 / 4 sets of tees

Par: 72

Open: Year-round

Tee times: Up to 7 days in advance

Green fees: $36 Monday through Thursday, $39 Friday, $48 Saturday and Sunday, including cart

Facility includes: Clubhouse, pro shop, driving range, chipping area, snack bar

Works with downtown hotels.

Missouri Bluffs Golf Club
18 Research Park Circle, St. Charles, MO 83304
314-939-6494
Public

Only 30 minutes from downtown, this challenging, long lay-out is perfect for those who enjoy hills and major elevation changes. Add some wooded fairways, and you have a difficult round on a rather new, scenic, high-end public facility.

Yardage: 5,197 to 7,047 / 5 sets of tees

Par: 71

Open: Year-round

Tee times: Up to 4 days in advance

Green fees: $85 weekdays, $105 weekends, including cart

Facility includes: Clubhouse, pro shop, driving range, chipping area, putting green, restaurant

Normandie Park Golf Club
7605 St. Charles Rock Road, St. Louis, MO 63133
314-862-4884
Public

"The oldest public golf club west of the mighty Mississippi" is how they promote this fun, tree-lined course that sees a great deal of play, including plenty of local tournaments. Some hills, well-bunkered greens, and a long par 3, 250-yard finish-ing hole characterize this fun, old layout.

Yardage: 5,943 to 6,534 / 2 sets of tees

Par: 71

Open: Year-round

Tee times: Up to 7 days in advance

Green fees: $20 to walk, $30 to ride Monday through Thursday; $26 to walk, $36 to ride Friday; $29 to walk, $39 to ride on weekends

Facility includes: Clubhouse, pro shop, driving range, putting green, deli

Spencer T. Olin Community Golf Course
4701 College Avenue, Alton, IL 62002
618-465-3111
Public

A top rated community course only 40 minutes northeast in neighboring Illinois, Olin has tons of trees but is still somewhat open with two lakes and plenty of well-placed traps. The long Arnold Palmer layout is very challenging with immaculate fairways on route to bent-grass greens that will test your putting game.

Yardage: 5,049 to 6,941 / 3 sets of tees

Par: 72

Open: Year-round

Tee times: Up to 14 days in advance

Green fees: $43 Monday through Thursday, $51 Friday, $57 Saturday and Sunday, including cart

Facility includes: Clubhouse, pro shop, driving range, putting green, restaurant

Packages with Alton Holiday Inn and Comfort Inn.

Quail Creek Golf Course
6022 Wells Road, St. Louis, MO 63128
314-487-1988
Public

Quail Creek features Bermuda fairways leading to bent-grass greens. The tight, challenging course has some water, long par 4s, and its share of hills—but is quite walkable. Only 20 minutes from downtown St. Louis, Quail encourages soft spikes by providing a $5 discount for golfers wearing them.

Yardage: 5,243 to 6,980 / 4 sets of tees

Par: 72

Open: Year-round

Tee times: Up to 7 days in advance

Green fees: $49 weekdays, $54 weekends, including cart

Facility includes: Clubhouse, pro shop, driving range, snack bar

Salt Lake City

The Salt Lake City area is home to two dozen scenic courses, many playing along hills and mountainsides. The views can be spectacular, so a camera should be part of your golf equipment. Weather permitting, golf is played from March through November.

Downtown hotels can probably help you more than any central tourist authority. You'll find brochures, magazines, and other information at pro shops and occasionally available through hotel concierge desks. The six 18-hole city courses book through a central number (fully automated, no humans available to answer questions), 801-484-3333.

Bonneville Golf Course
954 Connor Street, Salt Lake City, UT 84108
801-484-3333 tee times
801-583-9513
Public

Bonneville is a hilly, old tree-lined course that is not too tight but challenges you to keep the ball on the fairway nonetheless. The tough 70-year-old layout with fast tough greens is one of the most well-traveled, well-liked courses in the area.

Yardage: 5,861 to 6,824 / 3 sets of tees

Par: 72

Open: March through November

Tee times: Up to 7 days in advance

Green fees: $20, cart $5 extra per person.

Facility includes: Clubhouse, pro shop, chipping area, 2 putting greens, restaurant

Bountiful Ridge
2490 South Bountiful Boulevard, Bountiful, UT 84911
801-298-6040
Public

Taking a 15-minute trip to Bountiful, you'll find that this hill-side city course plays longer than it really is. It's not an easy layout for walking, but the Ridge is a fun course for players at all levels as you work your way around, over, or through a lot of big trees and some water to greens that tend to be fast in the hot weather. The course also sports some of the best scenic views in the state.

Yardage: 5,090 to 6,523 / 4 sets of tees

Par: 72/71

Open: March to November

Tee times: Up to 1 day in advance on weekdays, prior Thursdays for weekends

Green fees: $18 (cart $9 extra per person)

Facility includes: Clubhouse, pro shop, putting green, restaurant

Eaglewood Golf Course
1110 East Eaglewood Drive, North Salt Lake City, UT 84954
801-299-0088
Public

If you like hills, this one's for you. This challenging, scenic hillside course with a narrow back nine has some water holes and tricky greens. One of the newest courses in the area, Eaglewood sits only 15 minutes north of downtown.

Yardage: 5,173 to 6,772 / 3 sets of tees

Par: 71

Open: March through November

Tee times: Up to 2 days in advance

Green fees: $20 (cart $10 extra per person)

Facility includes: Clubhouse, pro shop, driving range, putting green, restaurant

Hotels can arrange bookings.

Mountain Dell Golf Course
3287 Cummings Road, Salt Lake City, UT
801-484-3333 tee times
801-582-3812 course
Public

Two courses, the Canyon and the Lakes, offer mountainside golf in a picturesque setting. The Canyon course requires more accuracy as you play along hills and through canyons. The Lakes course is wide open but also has its share of major elevation changes. Spanning some four hilly miles, both courses are fun and challenging. They also offer photo opportunities of passing deer, elk, moose, eagles, and perhaps a cougar or two.

Yardage: Canyon, 5,447 to 6,787, Lakes, 5,066 to 6,709 / 4 sets of tees each

Par: Canyon, 72, Lakes, 73

Open: March through November

Tee times: Up to 7 days in advance

Green fees: $20 (cart $10 extra per person)

Facility includes: Clubhouse, pro shop, driving range, putting green, restaurant

Riverbend Golf Course
12800 South 1040 West, Riverton, UT 84065
801-253-3673
Public

Elevation changes, sand and water hazards, and waste bunkers running the full length of fairways define this riverside course complete with marshlands and wild life. Only 15 minutes from downtown, Riverbend offers a little of everything that makes a good test of golf.

Yardage: 5,081 to 6,978 / 4 sets of tees

Par: 72

Open: Year-round

Tee times: Up to 2 days in advance

Green fees: $18 Monday through Friday, $20 weekends (cart $9.50 extra per person)

Facility includes: Clubhouse, pro shop, driving range, putting green, restaurant

Hotels can help book tee times and frequently send groups.

South Mountain Golf Club
1247 East Rambling Road, Draper, UT 84020
801-495-0500
Public

South Mountain is a brand new facility sporting a unique links course on the side of a mountain. No water, but rolling hills, mounding, and large multi-tiered greens await on a well-designed layout that utilizes the topography very well. The valley-situated course is a short 25-minute drive from Salt Lake City.

Yardage: 5,100 to 7,100 / 5 sets of tees

Par: 72

Open: Year-round

Tee times: Up to 7 days in advance

Green fees: $55 Monday through Thursday, $75 Friday through Sunday, including cart

Facility includes: Clubhouse, pro shop, driving range, chipping area, putting green, restaurant

Works with some local Draper-area hotels.

West Ridge Golf Course
5055 South West Ridge Boulevard, West Valley City, UT 84118
801-966-GOLF
Public

Just outside of Salt Lake City is this relatively new course with undulating hills, some narrow fairways, fast greens, and great views of the city. Not as well known as some of the city courses, West Ridge offers a fun round of golf and great views.

Yardage: 5,027 to 6,734 / 4 sets of tees

Par: 71

Open: Year-round

Tee times: Up to 7 days in advance

Green fees: $20 to $25 weekdays, $27 weekends, including cart

Facility includes: Clubhouse, pro shop, driving range, putting green, snack bar

Wingpointe Golf Course
3602 West 199 North, Salt Lake City, UT 84122
801-484-3333
Public

Wingpointe is a links-style golf course with several forced carries. If you like trees, forget it; this one is wide open with plenty of interesting terrain, including native grasses and many bunkers plus bent-grass greens. An excellent opportunity for anyone staying near Salt Lake City International Airport, the course is just off the runway. Hitting a plane will cost you a stroke.

(Wingpointe Golf Course cont'd)

Yardage: 5,228 to 7,100 / 4 sets of tees

Par: 72

Open: Year-round

Tee times: Up to 1 week in advance after 9 p.m.

Green fees: $20 walking, $30 riding

Facility includes: Clubhouse, pro shop, driving range, chipping area, 2 putting greens, restaurant

San Antonio

Many golfers consider San Antonio to be the jewel of the state. The hilly terrain produces exciting elevation changes, and architects have designed some marvelous courses for both resorts and public play.

La Cantera and the Quarry are among the best known public facilities in the state. Golfers play almost year-round and find it a bit easier than in Houston or Dallas to get on the courses, with new ones constantly being built in and around the city.

Flying L Ranch Golf Course
P.O. Box 1959, Bandera, TX 78003
210-460-3001
800-646-5407
Resort/Public

This is a hillside country course with a strong western theme offering beautiful scenic views. An hour outside of San Antonio, the partially tree-lined, 18-hole layout is moderate difficulty, offering 26 bunkers and 7 water holes.

Yardage: 5,442 to 6,646 / 3 sets of tees

Par: 72

Open: Year-round

Tee times: Up to 7 days in advance or when making room reservation

Green fees: $21.50 weekdays, $27.50 weekends, including cart

Facility includes: Clubhouse, pro shop, driving range, putting green, grill, conference center

Packages with resort.

La Cantera Golf Club

16641 La Cantera Parkway, San Antonio, TX 78256

210-558-GOLF

800-4-GOLF-US

Resort

The relatively new resort course features 75 bunkers, 6 natural water hazards, and half a dozen holes with panoramic views of San Antonio. While playing the long course, you'll find several streams, mature trees, and a stone quarry area. Sitting on some 200 acres, both the course and resort are among the highest rated in the large state.

Yardage: 5,000 to 7,100 / 5 sets of tees

Par: 72

Open: Year-round

Tee times: Up to 30 days in advance

Green fees: $75 Monday through Thursday, $90 Friday through Sunday, including cart

Facility includes: Clubhouse, pro shop, driving range, practice bunkers, putting green, restaurant

Packages with forthcoming Westin hotel.

Lady Bird Johnson Municipal Golf Course

Highway 16 South, Fredericksburg, TX 78624

830-997-4010

Public

An inexpensive, fun course, Lady Bird sits just 70 miles north of San Antonio. The 30-year-old course is tree-lined with

(Ladybird Johnson Municipal Golf Course cont'd)

three lakes on the back nine. It's also somewhat hilly with a creek running through several of the holes.

Yardage: 5,094 to 6,448 / 4 sets of tees

Par: 72

Open: Year-round

Tee times: Call Monday after 8:00 a.m. to book for the week

Green fees: $11 Monday through Friday, $17.50 weekends (cart $8.50 extra per person)

Facility includes: Clubhouse (under construction), pro shop, driving range, chipping area, putting green, snack bar

---

Pecan Valley Golf Club
4700 Pecan Valley Drive, San Antonio, TX 78223
210-333-9018
800 336-3418
Public

Pecan Valley is a classically designed golf course with mature trees lining straight and narrow fairways—a high degree of difficulty from the back tees. The 1968 PGA championship was held here. The course will be renovated in early 1999 while the new clubhouse is being built.

Yardage: 5,621 to 7,071 / 3 sets of tees

Par: 71

Open: Year-round

Tee times: Up to 7 days in advance if in their computer database; otherwise, up to 5 days in advance with Social Security number

Green fees: New fee structure after renovation

Facility includes: Clubhouse (forthcoming), pro shop, driving range, putting green, restaurant, snack bar, conference room

The Quarry Golf Club
444 East Basse Road, San Antonio, TX 78209
210-824-4500
Public

One of the best known courses in Texas, the Quarry is a links-style layout with a back nine that appropriately plays through a quarry. While awed by the scenic beauty of the course, you may also find yourself intimidated by forced carries over ravines. Long par 3s and 4s, plenty of bunkers, and some water lead to varying sizes of Bermuda greens. As most golfers in Texas will tell you, the Quarry is a first-rate golfing experience.

Yardage: 4,897 to 6,740 / 4 sets of tees

Par: 71

Open: Year-round

Tee times: Up to 30 days in advance

Green fees: $75 weekdays, $85 weekends, including cart

Facility includes: Clubhouse, pro shop, driving range, sand practice area, putting green, restaurant

Packages with Marriott and other area hotels.

San Diego
The temperature is always perfect for golf, and the courses are first-class, well-manicured, beautiful layouts varying in style. Nearly 40 courses are playable without membership in the immediate San Diego vicinity. Because golf is a main feature of the area, hotels are accommodating when it comes to booking tee times; many also offer packages or discounts. Scenic is an understatement for the courses in the area, many of which sport ocean views.

Some key phone numbers when visiting the area include the city course reservation system, 619-570-1234, M & M Tee Times, 619-456-8366, and the golf guide, 800-651-WAVE. The McIntosh Company also publishes the local golf map, available in nearly 500 area hotels or by calling 760-929-8685.

Carlton Oaks Country Club
9200 Inwood Drive, Santee, CA 92071
619-448-8500
Resort

Only 20 minutes from downtown San Diego, this Pete Dye layout incorporates narrow fairways, bent-grass greens, and plenty of water from both a creek and a lake into your golf outing. The highly rated course also sees a lot of tournament activity.

Yardage: 4,548 to 7,088 / 5 sets of tees

Par: 72

Open: Year-round

Tee times: Up to 7 days in advance or when making hotel reservations

Green fees: $65 weekdays, $75 weekends, including cart

Facility includes: Clubhouse, pro shop, driving range, chipping area, 2 putting greens, restaurant and banquet facility, snack bar

Various golf packages are offered with the 60-room lodge, in addition to deals to play other area courses.

Carmel Mountain Ranch Country Club
14050 Carmel Ridge Drive, San Diego, CA 92128
619-487-9224
Public

Built into a canyon, this scenic course plays longer than it appears. The design is tight with plenty of hills leading to small, fast greens. Forced carries and a fair number of hazards make this a good test. Carmel is 20 minutes from downtown San Diego.

Yardage: 5,228 to 6,130 / 4 sets of tees

Par: 71

Open: Year-round

Tee times: Up to 7 days in advance

Green fees: $65 weekdays, $75 weekends, including cart

Facility includes: Clubhouse, pro shop, driving range, chipping area, putting green, restaurant, snack bar

Makes arrangements through downtown San Diego hotels.

Coronado Golf Course
2000 Visalia Row, Coronado, CA 92118
619-435-3121
Public

Only a couple of miles from downtown, this is a flat, open, harbor-side course built on a landfill. Extremely popular, Coronado has its share of water holes leading to well-kept, tough greens. Outstanding views of the bay add to the charm.

Yardage: 5,784 to 6,633 / 3 sets of tees

Par: 72

Open: Year-round

Tee times: Up to 2 days in advance or up to 2 weeks in advance with $30 non-refundable fee

Green fees: $20 (cart $12 extra per person)

Facility includes: Clubhouse, pro shop, driving range, chipping area, putting green, restaurant, snack bar

Works with Marriott and all downtown hotels for tee times.

Eastlake Country Club
2375 Clubhouse Drive, Chula Vista, CA 91915
619-482-5757
Public

On 150 acres, the Eastlake course has 5 lakes (plus waterfalls) on a scenic open course with some undulation and bent-grass greens. Carts include a computerized yardage system to keep you abreast of where you are in relation to the green.

(Eastlake Country Club cont'd)

Yardage: 5,118 to 6,606 / 4 sets of tees

Par: 72

Open: Year-round

Tee times: Up to 7 days in advance

Green fees: $50 weekdays, $65 weekends, including cart

Facility includes: Clubhouse, pro shop, driving range, chipping areas, sand practice area, 2 putting greens, restaurant

Works with area hotels for tee times.

Four Seasons Aviara Golf Resort
7447 Batiquitos Drive, Carlsbad, CA 92009
760-603-6900
Resort

Native wildflowers and spectacular landscaping give you the feeling of playing through a garden, especially if you veer off the fairways. The beautiful Arnold Palmer course provides rolling hills, lakes, mounds, elevation changes, and even views of the Pacific Ocean. There's nothing more you could want from a course.

Yardage: 5,007 to 7,007 / 4 sets of tees

Par: 72

Open: Year-round

Tee times: Up to 6 days in advance

Green fees: $140, including cart

Facility includes: Clubhouse, awarding-winning pro shop, driving range, chipping area, putting green, restaurants

Ask about packages with resort.

Pala Mesa Resort
2001 Old Highway 395, Fallbrook, CA 92028
800-722-4700
619-728-5881
www.palamesa.com
Resort/Public

Just an hour north from San Diego, you'll find a beautiful course nestled in a scenic landscape. This resort layout plays along a creek and demands that you play strategic golf around trees and well-placed bunkers and along contoured fairways. The greens are very quick, challenging, and in pristine condition. Pala Mesa is well worth a drive up from San Diego or down from Los Angeles.

Yardage: 5,848 to 6,502 / 3 sets of tees

Par: 72

Open: Year-round

Tee times: Up to 7 days in advance or when reserving room

Green fees: Seasonal from $45 to $75, including cart

Facility includes: Clubhouse, pro ship, driving range, chipping area, putting green, four-star restaurant, snack bar

All-inclusive golf packages offered.

Rancho San Diego Golf Club
3121 Willow Glen Drive, El Cajon, CA 92019
619-442-9891
Public

A short drive from San Diego sit two courses designed for different levels of play. The Ivanhoe course is a long, challenging, open course, whereas the Monte Vista course is shorter, tighter, and geared more for higher handicappers. Both are scenic and well maintained.

(Rancho San Diego Golf Club cont'd)

Yardage: Ivanhoe, 5,792 to 6,649; Monte Vista, 5,761 to 6,600 / 3 sets of tees each

Par: 72

Open: Year-round

Tee times: Up to 4 days in advance

Green fees: $27 to $34, including cart

Facility includes: Clubhouse, pro shop, driving range, chipping area, putting green, restaurant, snack bar

---

Redhawk Golf Club
45100 Redhawk Parkway, Temecula, CA 92592
800-451-HAWK
909-695-1425
Semi-Private

In the middle of Southern California wine country is this intoxicatingly beautiful course. Redhawk has unique water holes in some amazing configurations, including an island green. You'll also enjoy lush vegetation, trees, sand, bunkers, and hazards of all kinds. The only thing this resort-style course is missing is the yellow brick road. (There is a cobblestone bridge.)

Yardage: 5,510 to 7,139 / 5 sets of tees

Par: 72

Open: Year-round

Tee times: Up to 7 days in advance

Green fees: $50 Monday through Thursday, $60 Friday, $75 Saturday and Sunday, including cart

Facility includes: Clubhouse, pro shop, driving range, chipping area, putting green, snack bar

Packages with Embassy Suites.

Riverwalk Golf Club
1150 Fashion Valley Road, San Diego, CA 92108
619-698-GOLF
Public

One of the area's newest facilities, Riverwalk features three 9-hole layouts with nearly 100 bunkers and water on 13 holes. The Presidio and Friars nines each feature tree-lined, undulating fairways, whereas the Mission course is flatter, shorter, and very scenic. From waterfalls and lakes to elevated greens and tees, these are three beautiful and challenging courses.

Yardage: 5,500 to 6,598, depending on configuration / 3 sets of tees

Par: 72

Open: Year-round

Tee times: Up to 7 days in advance

Green fees: $75 Monday through Thursday, $85 Friday, $95 Saturday through Sunday, including cart

Facility includes: Clubhouse, pro shop, driving range, chipping area, putting green, restaurant, snack bar

Hotel packages with several downtown San Diego hotels.

San Vincente Inn and Golf Course
24157 San Vincente Road, Romona, CA 92065
760-789-3477
Semi-Private

Thirty minutes northeast of San Diego, this course (and lodge) sits in a picturesque country setting. Rolling hills give a links flavor to the course, which requires straight but not necessarily long shots. Greens are in excellent condition.

Yardage: 5,543 to 6,210 / 3 sets of tees

Par: 72

Open: Year-round

(San Vincente Inn and Golf Course cont'd)

Tee times: Up to 5 days in advance, up to 1 year in advance for lodge guests

Green fees: $31 weekdays, $41 weekends (cart $14 extra per person)

Facility includes: Clubhouse, pro shop, driving range, chipping area, putting green, restaurant, snack bar

Country Inn offers packages.

Steele Canyon Golf Club
3199 Stonefield Drive, Jamul, CA 91935
619-441-6900
Public

Three different 9-hole courses, the Ranch, Meadows, and Canyon, let you pick and choose your 18-hole game. The Canyon course suits the name with many elevation changes on a tricky layout. The Ranch course plays long and flat through a working ranch, whereas the Meadow course features woodlands and streams. The scenic setting sits just 20 miles from downtown.

Yardage: 7,000, depending on configuration / 3 sets of tees

Par: 71 or 72, depending on configuration

Open: Year-round

Tee times: Up to 7 days in advance

Green fees: $50 Monday through Thursday, $60 Friday, $70 Saturday through Sunday, including cart

Facility includes: Clubhouse, pro shop, driving range, chipping area, putting green, restaurant, snack bar

Packages with downtown San Diego hotels.

Torrey Pines Golf Course
11480 North Torrey Pines Road, La Jolla, CA 92037
800-985-GOLF
Public

These two beautiful courses overlook the Pacific Ocean. Both courses see a great deal of tournaments and corporate activity. The North course is shorter and perhaps slightly easier than its neighbor to the south, which plays along the ocean and sees the PGA visit annually. This is municipal golf with a Pebble Beach ambiance.

Yardage: North, 6,118 to 6,326; South, 6,457 to 6,705 / 4 sets of tees

Par: 72

Open: Year-round

Tee times: Up to 60 days in advance

Green fees: $47 weekdays, $52 weekends (cart $28 extra)

Facility includes: Clubhouse, pro shop, driving range, chipping area, putting green, restaurant, snack bar

Course packages include those with personal course guides for three holes and various other amenities.

Twin Oaks Golf Course
1425 North Twin Oaks Valley Road, San Marcos, CA 92069
760-591-4700
Public

Twin Oaks is challenging for more advanced players, but playable for newer golfers. A well-designed layout, the course includes tight landing areas for long hitters and more room for shorter hitters. Some water comes into play along Bermuda grass fairways on route to bent-grass greens. The relatively new course, within 30 minutes of downtown, is not as well known...yet. The excellent practice facility includes one of the area's few grass driving ranges.

(Twin Oaks Golf Course cont'd)

Yardage: 5,423 to 6,535 / 3 sets of tees

Par: 72

Open: Year-round

Tee times: Up to 7 days in advance

Green fees: $44 weekdays, $49 Friday, $60 Saturday, $59 Sunday, including cart

Facility includes: Clubhouse, pro shop, driving range, chipping area, putting green, snack bar

Packages with Rancho Bernardo Inn and Temecula Creek Inn.

The Vineyard Golf Course
925 San Pasqual Road, Escondito, CA 92025
619-735-9545
Public

The Vineyard is a scenic mix of narrow front nine and open back nine. A lot of water comes into play en route to well-kept, tough greens. This fairly new course is less than 30 minutes north of downtown San Diego.

Yardage: 5,073 to 6,160 / 3 sets of tees

Par: 72

Open: Year-round

Tee times: Up to 7 days in advance

Green fees: $37 walking, $49 riding weekdays, $60 weekends, including cart

Facility includes: Clubhouse, pro shop, driving range, chipping area, putting green, restaurant, snack bar

San Francisco and Northern California

Often compared to New York, San Francisco (besides having more distinctive hills) also has limited space for golf courses. Therefore, you might want to venture outside of the city itself to some of the most famous, spectacular, scenic courses in the world located in Pebble Beach, Monterey Bay, Napa Valley, and other neighboring areas. Courses play along the bay and ocean, through mountains, or any place else where there are either dramatic elevation changes or ocean views to make the game exciting with spectacular views.

These high-end courses require that you plan well in advance. If you're taking a trip to Pebble Beach to spend a couple of days at one of the resorts, you can play more than one of the four championship courses on their resort package plans. Monterey Airport provides shuttles.

Between the standard but solid city layouts, such as Lincoln Park, Harding Park, and the famous high-end Pebble Beach resorts, nearly 80 courses of different styles are open to the public. Golf is played most of the year with wind the determining factor on some coastal courses.

Blue Rock Springs Golf Course
Columbus Parkway, Vallejo, CA 94951
707-643-8476
www.webfairway.com
Public

Blue Rock is home to two challenging 18-hole courses. The West is a short course with tree-lined fairways playing through a valley with some holes that have you climbing the surrounding hills. The East layout is a scenic, tricky course with well-placed bunkers and large greens. The courses sit 35 miles from San Francisco, and as homes to wildlife, they work to preserve the environment.

Yardage: West, 5,071 to 5,923; East, 4,851 to 6,064 / 3 sets of tees
Par: West 71; East 70
Open: Year-round
Tee times: Up to 7 days in advance for weekdays, from Tuesdays for weekends
Green fees: $ 24 to $ 28 depending on day and course (cart $24 extra, $17 for a single rider)
Facility includes: Clubhouse, pro shop, driving range, coffee shop, banquet facility

$4 discount rates for local residents.

Harding Park Golf Course
1 Harding Park Road, San Francisco, CA 94132
415-750-GOLF (city course tee time number)
Public

Basic, no-frills golf for those who are pressed for travel time but want a solid round of golf. The old, often crowded course still offers good golf on a well-treaded traditional layout. Along with Lincoln Park, Harding is one of a few small municipal courses.

Yardage: 6,205 to 6,743 / 3 sets of tees

Par: 72

Open: Year-round

Tee times: Up to 6 days in advance

Green fees: $26 weekdays, $31 weekends (cart $11 extra per person)

Facility includes: Clubhouse, driving range, 9-hole course, snack bar

City courses have resident cards available.

Indian Valley Golf Club
3035 Novato Boulevard, Novato, CA 94948
415-897-1118
Public

About 15 miles across the Golden Gate, Indian Valley is a scenic course with rolling hills on the fairways and plenty of trees all around. Elevation changes are dramatic to say the least; the course actually has an elevator to take you from the 13th green to the 14th tee.

Yardage: 5,238 to 6,253 / 3 sets of tees

Par: 72

Open: Year-round

Tee times: Up to 7 days in advance

Green fees: $27 Monday through Thursday, $32 Friday, $42 Saturday through Sunday (cart $11 extra per person)

Facility includes: Clubhouse, pro shop, driving range, putting greens, coffee shop

Lake Chabot Golf Course
11450 Golf Links Road, Oakland, CA 94605
510-351-5812
Public

If you like hills, this course is like playing through *The Sound of Music*. The up and down layout is Oakland's only municipal offering, providing wide open fairways, no water, and major elevation changes.

Yardage: 5,300 to 6,018 / 3 sets of tees

Par: 72

Open: Year-round

Tee times: Up to 7 days in advance for weekdays, prior Monday after 6 a.m. for weekends

Green fees: $18 Monday through Friday, $23 Saturday through Sunday (cart $18 extra weekdays, $22 weekends)

Facility includes: Driving range, putting green, restaurant, snack bar

The Links at Spanish Bay
2799 17 Mile Drive, Pebble Beach, CA 93953
408-647-7495
Resort/Public

One of the premiere golf resorts at Pebble Beach, Spanish Bay is an authentic seaside links (on a former sand mine) complete with mounds, dunes, water, wind, and spectacular ocean views. Tough greens add to the challenge on this world-renown facility, which is also a Certified Audubon Sanctuary Golf Course Signatory for its work in the area of ecology. The course is also a great place for spotting whales.

(The Links at Spanish Bay cont'd)

Yardage: 5,309 to 6,820 / 3 sets of tees

Par: 72

Open: Year-round

Tee times: Up to 30 days in advance, up to 1 year in advance for guests

Green fees: $185 walking, $210 riding, $165 including cart for guests

Facility includes: Clubhouse, pro shop, chipping area, putting green, restaurant

Packages with resort and three other area resorts; shuttle bus service to Monterey airport.

Napa Municipal Golf Course
Kennedy Park, 2295 Streblow Drive, Napa, CA 94958
707-255-4333
Public

A park course in the middle of wine country just over an hour from San Francisco, Napa is a championship-length course with rolling greens, tight fairways, and plenty of water. The walkable layout is both relaxing and scenic.

Yardage: 5,956 to 6,506 / 3 sets of tees

Par: 73/72

Open: Year-round

Tee times: Up to 7 days in advance

Green fees: $23 weekdays, $27 weekends (cart $11.50 extra per person)

Facility includes: Clubhouse, pro shop, driving range, putting greens, restaurant

Familiar to Napa hotels; works with discounts through www.webfairway.com.

Pasatiempo Golf Club
18 Clubhouse Road, Santa Cruz, CA 95060
408-459-9155
www.pastatiempo.com
Semi-Private

It doesn't get much better than this. Not as well known as Pebble Beach, this high-end course is on a *par*. Pasatiempo offers rolling fairways, treacherous bunkers, undulating greens, fabulous views of Monterey Bay, and an extremely challenging first-rate golfing experience from practice area to postround beverages. Much closer to San Jose, the course is about 90 minutes from downtown San Francisco.

Yardage: 5,647 to 6,483 / 3 sets of tees

Par: 72/71

Open: Year-round

Tee times: Up to 7 days in advance or prior Monday for weekend, up to 90 days in advance with $20 per person surcharge

Green fees: $115 Monday through Thursday, $125 Friday through Sunday (cart $17 extra per person)

Facility includes: Clubhouse, pro shop, driving range, chipping area, sand practice bunkers, putting green, restaurant, snack bar

Familiar to all area hotels.

Pebble Beach Golf Links
17 Mile Drive, Pebble Beach, CA 93953
408-624-3811
Resort/Public

If you're anywhere in California (and serious about golf), you should make the effort to play this world-famous course at least once. The enchanting 80-year-old layout hugs the coastline with spectacular ocean views and plenty of water on a links-style course perfectly laid out from tees to sloping

(Pebble Beach Golf Links cont'd)

greens. Pebble Beach is the height of golfing excellence along with its neighbors Spyglass and Spanish Links. Good luck getting on.

Yardage: 5,197 to 6,799 / 3 sets of tees

Par: 72

Open: Year-round

Tee times: 24 hours in advance or up to 18 months for hotel guests

Green fees: $295 (cart $25 extra per person), $255 for resort guests, including cart

Facility includes: Clubhouse, pro shop, driving range, chipping area, 2 putting greens, 9-hole par 3 course, restaurants

Ask about the resort packages, the shuttle to other three related courses, and the airport shuttle to Monterey Airport.

Spyglass Hill Golf Course
Spyglass Hill Road and Stevenson Drive, Pebble Beach, CA 93953
800-654-9300
408-654-9300
Resort/Public

Another of the fearsome foursome at Pebble Beach, Spyglass is also a sensational top-rated layout. Hills, sand, water, trees, ocean holes, and even caddies ($45 per bag) provide everything you could possibly want from a course—and the resort is first rate.

Yardage: 5,642 to 6,855 / 3 sets of tees

Par: 72

Open: Year-round

Tee times: Up to 14 days in advance secured; 72-hour cancellation policy for guests when making reservation

Green fees: $225 (cart $25 extra per rider), $195 for resort guests, including cart

Facility includes: Clubhouse, pro shop, driving range, putting green, restaurant, caddies

Hotel works with three other Pebble Beach resorts, offering shuttle buses to play all four courses and a shuttle to Monterey Airport.

Seattle/Tacoma

When it's not raining, Seattle is a great place for golf. Downtown hotel concierges can help set you up with a tee time, or Convention Services Northwest can put together outings. The Golf Network, 206-301-0472, is also at your disposal.

The game is growing rapidly with more than 15 new courses opening in the past couple of years. Most Seattle courses encompass wetlands and wildlife in tranquil settings within an hour of the Space Needle. Basking in the shadow of neighboring mountain ranges, golfers enjoy the game in the spring and summer months with some playing into and through the fall.

Harbour Pointe Golf Club
11817 Harbour Point Boulevard, Mukilteo, WA 98275
800-233-3128
Public

Only 20 minutes north of Seattle is the scenic Harbour Point course with a flat, watery front nine and a dryer, hilly back nine. Greens are large and the nine-year-old course is one of the best manicured in the state.

Yardage: 4,842 to 6,862 / 3 sets of tees

Par: 72

Open: Year-round

Tee times: Up to 7 days in advance

Green fees: Seasonal $35 to $47 plus cart ($13 per person)

Facility includes: Clubhouse, pro shop, driving range, chipping facility, 2 putting greens, restaurant

Works with concierge desks at downtown Seattle hotels.

Jackson Park Golf Course
1000 NE 135th Street, Seattle, WA 98125
800-892-8605 tee times
206-363-4747
Public

In the Olympic Hills section of Seattle, Jackson Park has an 18-hole championship course and a 9-hole par 3. This fun course has wide fairways and small greens and is a challenging walk in the park, literally.

Yardage: 5,636 to 6,212 / 4 sets of tees

Par: 71/74

Open: Year-round

Tee times: Up to 7 days in advance at the course, up to 6 days in advance by phone

Green fees: $18.50 (cart $20 extra)

Facility includes: Clubhouse, pro shop, putting green, chipping facility, snack bar

Several hotels, including nearby Embassy Suites, work with course.

Jefferson Park Golf Club
4101 Beacon Avenue South, Seattle, WA 98108
206-301-0472
Public

Jefferson Park varies in terrain from flat to hilly and sits smack dab in Seattle. A short, basic layout, the course from 1912 has been well maintained over the years and has seen a lot of great golfers. An accompanying par-3 layout is also fun, and both courses offer scenic city views.

Yardage: 5,440 to 6,093 / 3 sets of tees

Par: 73/70

Open: Year-round

Tee times: Up to 6 days in advance

Green fees: $18.50 (cart $20 extra)

Facility includes: Pro shop, driving range, chipping facilities, putting green, restaurant, snack bar

Lake Spanaway Golf Course
15602 Pacific Avenue, Tacoma, WA 98444
253 -531-3660
Public

A long, busy public facility, this is a well-kept course complete with its share of hazards and fir trees. Rated as one of the more challenging public courses in the Northwest, Lake Spanaway sits in nearby Tacoma.

Yardage: 5,459 to 6,938 / 4 sets of tees

Par: 74/72

Open: Year-round

Tee times: Up to 7 days in advance

Green fees: $20 (cart $20 extra)

Facility includes: Clubhouse, pro shop, driving range, chipping area, putting green, restaurant

North Shore Golf Club
4101 Northshore Boulevard Northeast, Tacoma, WA 98422
800-447-1375 tee times
253-927-1375
Semi-Private

North Shore is a scenic facility with a little of everything, including rolling terrain, nine lakes, more than 50 bunkers, tree-lined fairways, and a terrific practice facility. The course is well situated on the northeast end of Tacoma, only 45 minutes from Seattle.

Yardage: 5,442 to 6,305 / 3 sets of tees

Par: 71

Open: Year-round

(North Shore Golf Club cont'd)

Tee times: Up to 7 days in advance

Green fees: Seasonal from $22 to $34 (cart $24 extra)

Facility includes: Clubhouse, pro shop, driving range, chipping area, putting green, restaurant and banquet facility

$80 per year membership.

Port Ludlow Golf Course
751 Highland Drive, Port Ludlow, WA 98365
800-455-0272 tee times
360-437-0272
Resort/Public

Three nines make up this golf course on the bay, complete with fabulous views and a marina. The Tide course plays along the water, the Timber is tree-lined, and the Trail is target golf (and the most challenging of the three). From wetlands to wildlife, this course is designed to provide a host of hazards. A short ferry ride away, the courses are only 40 minutes from the Space Needle.

Yardage: 5,598 to 6,787 / 4 sets of tees

Par: 72

Open: Year-round

Tee times: Up to 5 days in advance or up to 6 months in advance for guests of the resort or inn

Green fees: Seasonal from $29 to $55 (cart $14 extra per person)

Facility includes: Clubhouse, pro shop, driving range, 2 putting greens, deli

The Heron Beach Inn and Port Ludlow Conference Center and Resort flank the course and offer 10% discounts.

West Seattle Golf Course
4470 35th Avenue Southwest, Seattle, WA 98126
206-935-5187
Public

Almost 60 years old, West Seattle is a hilly course with tree-lined fairways, a creek (in play on six holes), and panoramic views of downtown Seattle. The course is popular with visitors because of the views and easy accessibility, and it provides a challenge to various levels of players.

Yardage: 5,700 to 6,000 / 4 sets of tees

Par: 72

Open: Year-round

Tee times: Up to 7 days in advance in person, up to 6 days in advance by phone

Green fees: $18.50, $15 twilight, $10 late rate (cart $20 extra, plus $10 key deposit)

Facility includes: Clubhouse, pro shop, chipping and putting practice, snack bar

Willows Run Golf Course
10442 Willows Road, Redmond, WA 98052
425-883-1200
Public

An old-fashioned Irish-style links course, Willow Run has plenty of wetlands that strongly encourage you to stay on the fairways. As is the case with links courses, the wind will play defense most of the time. Large, tough greens—including the multi-tiered variety—will test your putting. The course also has yard markers, which are helpful on a wide-open course where it is easy to misread the distance to the green.

Yardage: 5,435 to 6,851 / 3 sets of tees

Par: 72

Open: Year-round

(Willows Run Golf Course cont'd)

Tee times: Up to 7 days in advance

Green fees: $35 weekdays, $45 weekends (cart $24 extra)

Facility includes: Clubhouse, pro shop, driving range, chipping area, putting green, restaurant, snack bar

Washington, D.C.

Washington, D.C.

The nation's capital has a lot of historic sites but room for only a few golf courses. Three public city courses, Rock Creek, East Potomac, and Langston, sit in D.C. itself, but more golfing activity takes place in neighboring Maryland and Virginia.

New courses are popping up, and concierges at some of the downtown hotels are slowly getting information on them. Playing golf in D.C., however, requires a little investigative snooping. This section contains a mix of courses from urban layouts to top new high-end facilities that are typical of the area. The peak season for golf in D.C. runs from April through October, but as long as the winter weather stays away, you can keep on playing.

Bristow Manor Golf Club
11507 Valley View Drive, Bristow, VA 20136
703-368-3558
Public

Less than an hour south of D.C., Bristow serves up an open links-style course complete with marshlands, mounds, tricky rough areas, and plenty of wind. Water from creeks and ponds come into play on several holes of this challenging new (six-year-old) course.

Yardage: 5,154 to 7,100 / 4 sets of tees

Par: 74/72

Open: Year-round

Tee times: Up to 7 days in advance

Green fees: $39 Monday through Thursday, $69 Friday through Sunday, including cart

Facility includes: Clubhouse, pro shop, driving range, chipping area, putting green, restaurant, historic mansion with banquet facilities

East Potomac Golf Course
Ohio Drive South West, Washington, DC 20024
202-863-9011
Public

One of three sister-city public courses, along with Langston and the shorter, hilly Rock Creek, East Potomac sits near the famed river and in the shadow of the Jefferson Memorial. Perfect for politicians, the course has few obstacles to hinder your day. In fact, it's a fairly flat, no-frills layout with a mixed variety of greens—some small, some large, and some sloping.

Yardage: 5,300 to 6,619 / 4 sets of tees

Par: 72

Open: Year-round

Tee times: First come, first serve

Green fees: $15 weekdays, $19 weekends (cart $18 extra)

Facility includes: Clubhousepro shop, double-deck driving range, 4 putting greens, snack bar

Harbourtowne Golf Resort and Country Club
Route 33 and Martingham Drive, St. Michaels, MD 21663
410-475-5183
800-446-9066
Semi-Private/Public

A semi-private resort and public facility, if that makes any sense, Harbourtowne invites visitors to play three times until you must join. A relatively flat course, the Pete Dye layout is tough with a lot of well-placed bunkers, some tight and some open holes, bent-grass fast greens, plus great scenery. An hour and a half away from D.C., the course is popular with corporate travelers.

Yardage: 5,030 to 6,320 / 4 sets of tees

Par: 71/70

Open: Year-round

Tee times: Up to 6 months in advance

Green fees: $59, $49 for hotel guests, $47 for corporate groups, including cart

Facility includes: Clubhouse, pro shop, driving range, chipping area, putting green, snack bar

Resort discounts and membership.

Langston Golf Course
2600 Benning Road Northeast, Washington, DC 20002
202-397-8638
Public

One of the few city courses, Langston is a solid layout with 36 bunkers mostly surrounding greens, some water holes, and a river running through the course. No, you probably won't see

(Langston Golf Course cont'd)

many high-ranking officials on Langston, but you'll have fun on this easily accessible course.

Yardage: 6,340 / 3 sets of tees

Par: 71

Open: Year-round

Tee times: First come, first serve

Green fees: $15 weekdays, $18 weekends (cart $18 extra)

Facility includes: Clubhouse, pro shop, driving range, putting green, snack bar

---

Landsdowne Golf Club
44050 Woodbridge Parkway, Landsdowne, VA 20176
800-541-4801
703-729-4071
Resort/Public

Two diverse nines make up this excellent course, just shy of an hour from the capital. The links-style front nine is wide open with typical links mounds and trouble. The back nine heads into tree-lined, tighter territory. Some tough par 3s and elevation changes round out this long Virginia course.

Yardage: 5,213 to 7,057 / 4 sets of tees

Par: 72

Open: Year-round

Tee times: Up to 5 days in advance for weekdays, up to 2 days in advance for weekends

Green fees: $80 weekdays, $90 weekends, including cart

Facility includes: Clubhouse, pro shop, driving range, chipping area, putting green, restaurant, deli

Packages with resort.

Pleasant Valley Golf Course
4750 Pleasant Valley Road, Chantilly, VA 20151
703-631-7904
Semi-Private

Thirty minutes from D.C. is this new spacious Tom Clark layout in a vast park setting. Large sculptured bunkers and some hills appear with water on several holes. The front is tree-lined, but the back nine opens up somewhat. Bent grass from tees to good-sized greens, this Pleasant Valley course is a pleasant escape from busy D.C.

Yardage: 5,083 to 6,957 / 4 sets of tees

Par: 72

Open: Year-round

Tee times: Up to 7 days in advance

Green fees: $55 Monday through Thursday, $60 Friday, $70 weekends, including cart

Facility includes: New clubhouse, driving range, chipping areas, putting green, restaurant

Works with Westfield Marriott.

Redgate Municipal Golf Course
14500 Avery Road, Rockville, MD 20853
301-309-3055
Public

Some trees, a little water, and a lot of hills characterize Redgate, a public course only 20 minutes outside of downtown D.C. The not-too-long course features fast greens and is a tough layout, good for all levels of golfers.

Yardage: 5,271 to 6,400 / 4 sets of tees

Par: 71

Open: Year-round

(Redgate Municipal Golf Course cont'd)

Tee times: Monday for weekends; otherwise, first come, first serve

Green fees: $24 Monday through Thursday, $27 Friday through Sunday (cart $23 extra)

Facility includes: Clubhouse, pro shop, short (irons) driving range, putting green, snack bar

---

South River Golf Links

3451 Solomons Island Road, Edgewater, MD 21037

800-767-4837

410-798-5865

Public

South River is a new course cut out of a mature hardwood forest with isolated bent-grass fairways on a somewhat mountainous terrain. Some severe elevation changes plus carefully placed bunkers and ponds make this layout both demanding and forgiving.

Yardage: 4,935 to 6,723 / 4 sets of tees

Par: 72

Open: Year-round

Tee times: Call 1 week ahead at noon

Green fees: $40 to walk, $50 to ride weekdays; $60 to walk or ride on weekends

Facility includes: Clubhouse, pro shop, driving range, putting green, snack bar

Appendix

Other Courses

Below are three courses that do not belong to major markets but should be included because they are among the premiere golf resorts in the country, or the world, for that matter.

Coeur D'Alene Resort Golf Course

900 Floating Green Drive, Coeur D'Alene, ID 83814

208-667-4653

Resort

It's hard to find a more beautiful, scenic course anywhere; bring a camera. This top-rated resort course includes the often photographed, famed floating island green, accessible only by boat. Primarily a links-style layout, the challenging high-end course has a little of everything with well-placed trees, water, and bunkers. There are also some elevation changes as you play around and sometimes over the lake. The nearest major city is Spokane, Washington, which is 45 minutes west.

Yardage: 4,446 to 6,309 / 4 sets of tees

Par: 71

Open: Year-round

Tee times: Up to 3 days in advance, guests when booking reservation

(Coeur D'Alene Resort Golf Course cont'd)

Green fees: $135 to $180, including cart and forecaddie

Facility includes: Clubhouse, pro shop, driving range, putting green, restaurant

Packages with resort.

Pinehurst Resort and Country Club
Carolina Vista Drive, Village of Pinehurst, NC 28374
910-295-6811
Resort

Open before the turn of the last century, Pinehurst moves into the next century as the resort most synonymous with the game of golf. Eight courses make up this golfing Mecca, which includes everything the game can offer on 144 holes. The #2 course is considered the cream of the crop. The Donald Ross gem will be home to the 1999 U.S. Open Championship. Long accurate drives and iron shots are necessary to reach tiny greens on this perfectly contoured design. Pinehurst #1 is a manageable tight-wooded layout with small greens demanding pinpoint accuracy. The #3 is a short course sitting securely in the woods with rolling fairways, water, and plenty of doglegs on route to small greens. The #4 was revamped in 1973 and requires careful shot preparation to larger greens than its neighbors, whereas #5 leads the pack in water with several ponds and lakes. The #6 is a long course with woods, thick vegetation, water, and mounds, and #7 is tighter, dryer, and wooded with severely rolling terrain. The new course, #8, has narrow fairways and elevation changes and provides a solid golf outing.

Yardage: #1, 5,329 to 5,853; #2, 5,966 to 7,020; #3, 5,198 to 5,956; #4, 5,969 to 6,878; #5, 5,658 to 6,827; #6, 5,430 to 7,098; #7, 4,924 to 7,114; #8, 5,177 to 7,092 / 3 to 5 tee areas per course

Par: #1, 73/70; #2, 74/72; #3 72/70; #4, 73/72; #5, 73/72; #6, #7, and #8, 72

Open: Year-round

Tee times: Non-resort guest, day of; guests, when booking reservations

Green fees: #2, $225; #7, $190; #8, $200; #s1, 3, 4, 5, and 6, $140, including cart

Facility includes: Clubhouses, pro shops, driving ranges, chipping areas, putting greens, restaurants, snack bars

Packages available.

Treetops Sylvan Resort
3962 Wilkinson Road, Gaylord, MI 48735
800-444-6711
888-Treetops
Resort/Public

Four outstanding courses by top designers make this one of the most renowned golf resorts. The Robert Trent Jr. Masterpiece course is considered the toughest with undulating, narrow fairways that aren't forgiving as they slope toward the sides into the rough. The demanding, scenic, long layout includes its share of bunkers and water holes and forces you to use every club in your bag. The Rick Smith Signature and brand new Tradition courses are both player friendly. The Signature sports numerous bunkers, some major elevation changes, and great views. The Tradition is walkable, wide open, and more forgiving. The challenging Fazio Premier course has a well laid-out variety of holes with wide fairways and well-placed bunkers leading to some tough approach shots.

Treetops is an Audubon Signature course for its environmental preservation.

Yardage: Masterpiece, 4,972 to 7,060; Signature, 4,604 to 6653; Traditions, 4,907 to 6,467; Premier, 5,039 to 6,832 / Signature, 5 sets of tees; all others, 4 sets of tees

Par: Masterpiece, 72; Signature and Traditions, 71; Premier, 72

(Treetops Sylvan Resort cont'd)

Open: April through October

Tee times: Up to the year 2010 in advance

Green fees: $52 to $86 for non-guests (cart $15 extra per rider on Traditions, other courses include cart in green fees); $44 to $70 for resort guests (cart extra on Traditions), caddies also available on Traditions course only by advance reservation

Facility includes: Clubhouse, pro shop, 2 driving ranges, putting greens, restaurants at lodge

Several packages with lodge.

Index